The Content Driven Product Launch

Michael Passanante

Acknowledgements

The content marketing campaign that is the subject of this book was the result of the hard work of many dedicated individuals who gave their time and expertise to make it successful.

Jon Besler and Jim Hoffman provided the kind of backing from a senior leadership team that most marketers can only dream about. They recognized the value of our efforts and supported them vigorously. Jim was a major contributor and visionary behind both the Readmissions Analytics product and content for the campaign.

Thanks go out to Cyndy Kowalski who contributed an incredible amount of original content. Without her expertise and willingness to write this material, the campaign would never have reached its potential.

Thanks also to Laureen Rimmer who led the service line responsible for Readmissions Analytics and was an excellent partner throughout the campaign. And thanks to Dr. Ed Niewiadomski for his expert clinical input.

Contents

Disclaimer

This book is presented solely for educational purposes. The author and publisher are not offering it as legal, accounting, or other professional services advice. While best efforts have been used in preparing this book, the author and publisher make no representations or warranties of any kind and assume no liabilities of any kind with respect to the accuracy or completeness of the contents and specifically disclaim any implied warranties of merchantability or fitness of use for a particular purpose. Neither the author nor the publisher shall be held liable or responsible to any person or entity with respect to any loss or incidental or consequential damages caused, or alleged to have been caused, directly or indirectly, by the information or programs contained herein. Links to external websites are maintained by their respective users and are accurate at the time of this writing. No warranty may be created or extended by sales representatives or written sales materials. Every company is different and the advice and strategies contained herein may not be suitable for your situation. You should seek the services of a competent professional before beginning any program.

Introduction

In 2015, BESLER Consulting launched a new product named Readmissions Analytics. This product was intended to help hospitals deal with a new financial penalty that the Centers for Medicare and Medicaid Services (CMS) imposed on them for what they deemed as excess readmissions, that is, people being discharged from the hospital and then returning in less than thirty days over a certain threshold.

Over 2,600 hospitals received reduced Medicare payments due to excess readmissions in 2015. Each year, CMS provides every affected hospital with a data file so they can validate their readmission penalty calculation. The file is cumbersome to work with and does not include all of the information a hospital needs to evaluate the underlying causes of readmissions.

Readmissions Analytics provided access to a powerful, interactive tool that combined financial and clinical information, allowing hospitals to quickly and easily understand readmissions data in ways that would be impossible using the CMS-supplied data alone, so they can reduce their long-term exposure to Medicare penalties. It also included a deep-dive analysis from subject matter experts around data trends for certain factors that drove the penalty up or down.

Since this was a new product that dealt with a new problem, there were several challenges that needed to be overcome to gain marketplace acceptance, not the smallest of which was gaining the attention of decision makers and influencers in the crowded hospital space.

This book is the story of the content marketing campaign that launched this product into the marketplace.

The campaign was not developed in a bubble by the marketing department. It took the contributions of many internal experts to make it a success. It achieved quantifiable results for the business and was ultimately recognized by MarketingProfs when they awarded it the B2B Bright Bulb Award for Best Small In-House Campaign of 2015.

Throughout the course of this book, I will walk you through the steps taken to create and execute the campaign along with the thinking behind each one.

This book is not meant to be a complete guide to content marketing, nor is it intended to be a literal roadmap for how you should create your campaigns. I don't discuss every conceivable tactic you could employ; rather, I focus on those things that made sense in the context of this initiative.

For the greater part of the campaign, I was a marketing department of one. Still, with the contributions of a wider team and some very thoughtful execution, a campaign was deployed that became a force multiplier for the business.

Through telling the story of the Readmissions Analytics campaign, I've strived to illustrate how content marketing can be used to successfully launch a new product or service without a massive budget or unlimited resources. I hope this story inspires you, teaches you, and leaves you with a sense of optimism that you too can be successful with content marketing in your own business.

Let's get started!

Identify your business challenges

Before you begin to scope out your content marketing plan or even define your goals, you must spend some time exploring and documenting the business challenges that you plan to address with your program.

These challenges should be the driving force behind your content themes. They will also give you a variety of pathways and ideas for developing content.

Content marketing is excellent for educating your audience and building brand awareness. At a high level, this allows you to demonstrate value and build a relationship with your target audience.

Done well, your content can also help your audience overcome their fears, misperceptions, and objections around topics or even specific products and services. This is an extremely important component and not to be underestimated.

A great approach for determining the challenges you are likely to face is to use the framework developed by Oratium (www.oratium.com), called "Know-Believe-Do."

This is a waterfall process developed by their CEO, Tim Pollard, that you can work through to build the base of information you need. It can be helpful to begin with the end in mind and work backwards.

First, you identify the action that you wish your target

audience to take - the **do**. This could be as big as a purchase decision or as small as a click on a "download now" button.

Next, you'll consider what your audience must **believe** in order to take that action. For example, if they choose to purchase your offering, they must be confident that it will solve their problem. They may also need to believe that other alternatives will not solve their problem as well, as fast, or as cost-effectively. Or perhaps establishing beliefs around the reliability of your offering and your staff are key elements.

Once you know what they must believe, you can then determine what pieces of information they must **know** in order to develop those beliefs. This could come in the form of expert advice, customer testimonials, third-party data, product specifications and so on.

As you work through this exercise, list as many challenges as you can think of. You'll probably see that many of them will relate to each other in some way. From there, you can begin to group them under larger headings, the goal being to define a few major areas of concern that you need to address. Each sub-challenge can then be addressed in different aspects of your content marketing program.

Before you move forward with the planning process, share these challenges with other key stakeholders within your organization. Ensure that you are all aligned around the challenges you face and agree on which ones must be addressed and in which priority if possible.

Consider these questions as you work through the Know-

Believe-Do framework:

• Are my target customers familiar with my firm? My offering?

• What problems are my potential customers trying to solve?

• What are some of the knowledge gaps that exist in the market?

• Are there perceptions or misperceptions that should be addressed about my organization, my offering, or in the market generally?

• Are there different types of personas I need to reach? What will each persona need to know?

• What objections or concerns might my target audience have regarding my product or service?

• What will my prospects need to know to move from the status quo?

• What will my prospects need to know to change from a competitive offering to mine?

• Who do my customers trust?

• What types of proof do they consider valuable and valid?

How this applied to Readmissions Analytics

For the launch of Readmissions Analytics, the following challenges were defined:

• While BESLER Consulting was well known for healthcare financial expertise, the firm's reputation in the clinical space was not well established, making it a longer road to develop credibility for the new offering among clinical personas.

• The sales team needed to speak with new personas within the hospital in order to gain traction for the offering.

• Many healthcare professionals were not familiar with or utilizing the CMS data supplied to evaluate their penalties; this was the foundation for Readmissions Analytics.

• The perception among some healthcare financial professionals was that it would be more cost-effective to maintain the revenue for readmissions and just pay the Medicare penalty.

Admittedly, I did not learn about Tim's Know-Believe-Do framework until after this campaign. However, I think this approach is perhaps one of the best ways you can easily identify the communications challenges you'll face, and the messages you'll need to express in order to overcome them.

In the analysis below, I focus on the high-level Know and Believe aspects of the campaign. What we wanted prospects to **do** depended on the particular situation. For instance, we may have wanted them to download a content asset, accept a demo appointment, or make a purchase decision. You can easily apply Know-Believe-Do to even the smallest actions you want your prospects to take.

Looking back, I think this is how the Know-Believe-Do framework applied to the Readmissions Analytics launch challenges:

• While BESLER Consulting was well known for healthcare financial expertise, the firm's reputation in the clinical space was not well established, making it a longer road to develop credibility for the new offering among clinical personas. *[Current customers needed to **know** that BESLER possessed expertise in the clinical space so they could **believe** that we were capable of delivering the solution.]*

• The sales team needed to speak with new personas within the hospital in order to gain traction for the offering. *[New contacts within the hospitals needed to **know** who we were and what we could provide before they could **believe** that we could help solve their problems.]*

• Many healthcare professionals were not familiar with or utilizing the CMS data supplied to evaluate their penalties; this was the foundation for Readmissions Analytics. *[Potential customers needed to **know** about the value that the CMS data could provide before they could **believe** that it could benefit them and ultimately find utility in our offering.]*

• The perception among some healthcare financial professionals was that it would be more cost-effective to maintain the revenue for readmissions and just pay the

Medicare penalty. *[Potential customers needed to **know** why it would not be beneficial to continue paying penalties before they could **believe** that it would be worth purchasing a product to help them do so.]*

Define your audience

Now that you have documented the business challenges you must overcome to be successful, you need to specifically define who the target audience will be for your campaign.

This is a critical step for several reasons.

First, you need to figure out who has influence and/or decision-making authority in the purchase of your product or service. For complex services, there are often many individuals involved in making a purchase decision. Each one may have a different role within the company and will bring their own points of view to the table. They may be trying to solve the same problem, but will look at issues through their own lens based on their role.

Put another way, different individuals could derive different benefits from utilizing your offering. Their pain points, use cases, and expected involvement will all vary.

As we touched on earlier, beyond the benefits enjoyed from solving any particular issue, each person must also overcome their own fears, apprehensions, and personal allegiances before a consensus on a purchasing decision can be reached. Sometimes, you'll find that although there are many influencers involved in the process, no one person is willing to step up and make a decision or be your champion.

A good way to document these dynamics is by creating user personas. Personas examine each user role by establishing their pain points, typical job activities, potential personality traits, and influence or decision-making authority, among other things. Persona development can get incredibly detailed, but at a minimum you should attempt to document the needs and concerns of key roles you are likely to encounter during the typical buying process. It's also important to know what each person must accomplish to be seen as successful in their role.

As it relates to your content marketing initiatives specifically, you should also include the following types of elements in your persona profiles:

• Publications they read

• Websites they visit

• Social media platforms they engage on

• Conferences they attend

As you work through this process, you will begin to see where, if any, overlap exists between personas. When you get down to the process of mapping specific content deliverables, this will give you the knowledge you need to decide which deliverables map to each persona type and where you could promote them to get the most exposure.

Since different personas will likely need to receive different pieces of information on their Know-Believe-Do journey, you will have to be thoughtful as to how you can leverage different pieces of content across the campaign.

It is also important to consider the number and types of business verticals you'll encounter as you define your target audiences. This information is overlaid across your persona types and provides an additional dimension to your planning. If you market across verticals, this becomes particularly important as you decide which messages you deliver and to whom. It may be that certain pieces of content will work in any vertical. However, a more likely scenario is that you'll have to craft content that speaks to the challenges in each vertical.

Say, for example, your target persona is a marketing director. A marketing director in a large B2C company will probably have different needs, buyers, and use cases to address than a marketing director in a niche B2B company. They are both marketing directors, but their business focus and verticals make a major difference in the types of things they need to get their jobs done.

Your targets may be obvious based on the positioning of your offering. But if you have an offering that can stretch across personas and business verticals, then defining each dimension as clearly as you can will help you to construct meaningful content while showcasing it in the best possible venues.

How this applied to Readmissions Analytics

For Readmissions Analytics, the high-level target business vertical was pretty straightforward - hospitals. However, there were still some elements around the organization type that made a difference.

For instance, we were primarily looking for hospitals that had experienced a high first-year readmissions penalty. These hospitals represented the lowest hanging fruit. However, even hospitals that didn't have a penalty in the first year of the program could be subject to penalties in future years.

Hospitals in Maryland did not need to be targeted because they were excluded from the federal program. While there might have been some interaction as spillover from our content marketing efforts, these hospitals would not be the focus of any concerted sales efforts for obvious reasons.

Persona types represented a more pressing challenge.

The BESLER team was most familiar and comfortable dealing with hospital finance professionals. The Medicare readmissions penalties hit the bottom lines of their revenue streams directly, so they clearly had a reason to pay attention to the issue. However, the ability to impact the behaviors associated with reducing readmissions rested squarely on the shoulders of clinical and hospital quality professionals.

As you might imagine, this usually meant that readmissions was a cross-departmental issue that necessitated committees with representatives from various areas across the hospital to deal with the issue. While traditional finance contacts knew BESLER well and could provide introductions, the underlying data from Readmissions Analytics and associated findings would be leveraged by other groups who handled clinical implementation initiatives.

Moreover, readmissions had become a political hot potato within hospitals, meaning that no one group felt compelled to make decisions with regard to products like Readmissions Analytics. Also, influencers and decision-makers were often different from hospital to hospital, depending on how each organization was structured administratively.

The content marketing campaign therefore needed to address multiple personas while maintaining a consistent message throughout. Knowing who the key targets would be up front gave us the ability to construct deliverables that resonated with each target audience. It also allowed us to pick and choose the partners we would work with to syndicate and promote our content for optimal reach.

Establish your content marketing purpose and goals

Before you begin any content marketing campaign, you have to articulate goals.

There are two types of goals: strategic and tactical.

Strategic goals will go directly to your purpose: **the why**.

In theory, strategic goals should be relatively straightforward. You wouldn't be creating a campaign if you didn't have a strategic goal, right?

However, it's important to craft specific strategic goals that truly describe what you are trying to achieve. These should be big ideas that will move your business or initiative forward.

Before you proceed with any type of tactical planning, or tactical goal identification for that matter, you should ensure that key stakeholders are in agreement around your strategic goals. If there is any miscommunication or divergent opinions as to what your strategic goals should be, then chances are your tactical execution will fail to deliver on your purpose, at least to someone.

At the end of the day, all goals must eventually deliver revenue. But, in order to get there, you may have to deal with some very specific issues that will move the market along. Ideally, you've identified these issues from working through Chapter Two - Defining Your Business Challenges.

Michael Passanante

The hard part now is deciding which challenges you can or should address through content marketing.

Content marketing is not suitable for addressing every business challenge you might encounter. Moreover, if you try to do too much with your campaign, you risk diluting your message or delivering a disjointed or fragmented set of deliverables.

To be effective, all of your content must work in harmony. As such, you need to ensure that your content strategy is focused on a discrete set of goals that are clear and achievable. Simply put, this means that you understand, and all of your key stakeholders are aligned around, the purpose of your content marketing campaign.

If you fail to align around a purpose, you will inevitably end up having a difficult conversation with your stakeholders to justify the point of your campaign or content marketing in general.

Tactical goals can come in all shapes in sizes. As the term implies, they relate to the performance of specific tactics. You may not be able to build out tactical goals at the outset of your planning process, simply because you haven't worked through the tactics you'll be employing just yet.

Your selection of tactical goals is almost limitless. So many marketing activities can now be measured so precisely that it really comes down to selecting just those tactical goals and metrics that are key drivers for your business.

Just a few examples include:

The Content Driven Product Launch

• Downloads of assets like white papers

• Views of infographics or videos

• Social media engagement including shares and comments

• Conversions via specific web pathways

• Web page views

• Number of contacts or leads generated

• The number of appointments or demos generated

• Pipeline value built

There are many other very specific things you could measure. The key is deciding on the information you should be measuring in order to move the needle for your effort. You don't have to measure everything to have a good campaign.

At the end of every campaign, you'll be measuring revenue in some form. That's essentially a given. Revenue is the final result of any sales and marketing effort. Make sure you've established what your number needs to be and what you are specifically accountable for.

In a B2B situation, some revenue may be directly attributable to your content marketing efforts. Perhaps you have a solution that is self-service or sold via direct channels making revenue measurement much simpler.

If you're involved in a complex sale, the more likely scenario is that revenue attainment will be a joint effort between marketing and sales. Take the time up front to consider how marketing efforts will be tracked and attributed so you can measure and justify your efforts.

It can be hard to forecast specific, quantifiable goals around how different pieces of content will perform. Sometimes it is just difficult to know up front what will resonate, no matter how well you know your audience. There are also factors out of your control, like how well Google ranks blog posts, for instance.

Your first goal should be to be useful to your audience. If you start there, then you have a good chance of seeing your tactical goals come to fruition.

If you're interested in how to more specifically calculate the ROI of specific content marketing tactics, you might consider reading "The Content Formula: Calculate the ROI of Content Marketing & Never Waste Money Again" by Michael Brenner and Liz Bedor.

The bottom line is that it's impossible to know if you were successful if you don't set goals, so do it!

How this applied to Readmissions Analytics

After assessing the challenges faced for launching Readmissions Analytics, the following strategic goals were set:

• Begin a relationship with personas related to quality

initiatives who could champion our offering within hospitals.

• Cement our unique thought leadership position and establish our authority in the readmissions space.

• Familiarize healthcare professionals with the data required to properly analyze readmissions.

• Evangelize the true cost of readmissions, so healthcare professionals could understand the financial implications of reducing readmissions.

There are other things we could have tried to accomplish, but these goals were the ones we felt had the biggest potential to move the market and were best suited to be addressed through content marketing.

To be completely transparent about the process, we did not sit around in a room one day to hammer out this exact language in a structured process. As we had conversations with people in the market and began to see red flags pop up, we started down the road of addressing these concerns, piecemeal at first, and then in a more structured way. In other words, our strategic alignment happened somewhat organically as the challenges we faced became more evident.

The fluid nature of new product introductions makes this almost inevitable. The key is building a flexible approach and platform that allows you to pivot so you can address concerns as they arise.

In terms of tactical goals, we knew for sure that we wanted

to achieve 50 demos through sales and marketing efforts in the first six months post-launch. A relatively modest conversion rate from those demos would lead to achievement of the first-year revenue goal.

A goal was also set to get an article published in a major publication dealing with certain marketplace misperceptions about the readmissions issue.

Since we were not new to this vertical, but somewhat new to the problem of readmissions and the personas involved, putting goals around specific tactical assets was a bit trickier.

We looked at the performance of previous ebooks and webinars to benchmark where we thought we should be. This began to unfold as we put together the nuts and bolts of the tactical plan. As we moved through planning, it became more obvious where we needed to place our focus and when we might need to partner with third parties to help promote our message.

While we tracked a whole host of metrics during the campaign, the main focus for us would be downloads of assets. These downloads would help produce the specific leads we needed for us to reach the product demo goal.

Choose your hero content

Now that you have your goals set, it's time to decide what your hero content (or cornerstone content as it is sometimes called) will be. A good way to get started is by selecting the major themes you need to explore in order to support your campaign.

Your themes will usually cascade from your business challenges, as they will represent the areas you must address in order to make the needle move.

Think back to our earlier discussion. What do your customers need to know and believe in order to take action? Here is where you will operationalize those themes.

When we think about hero content, we generally think about one key asset that comprehensively addresses a theme.

For instance, you might decide that you need to answer one major question that your prospects are grappling with. Perhaps you answer their question in the form of an in-depth ebook. Once you have that ebook built, you can then pick and pull content from it to create shorter blog posts, Slideshare decks, podcasts, and more!

Having one comprehensive source at your disposal gives you a library of material to pull from that you can use to build any number of assets to support your initiative. You can dive deeper into sub-topics as you break up the content. And you give your audience the choice to select their preferred format for engaging with your information.

While it's often easier to begin with one large piece of hero content and then draw from that to create other deliverables, you can work in the opposite direction as well. For instance, after selecting a theme, you could record a series of podcasts and then combine the transcripts to create an ebook. The key is that you are staying on message while making the most of the content you create.

Establishing your hero content up front will help you do several things:

1. You will document your themes and stick to them.

2. You can avoid trying to do too much with one piece of hero content as you are focusing on a single theme.

3. You can achieve scale around a theme by breaking up hero content and delivering it piecemeal in other formats over time.

These points are important for any content marketing program, but they are especially important if you are a small or mid-size business. You must establish discipline to keep from drifting away from your core themes. And you have to squeeze as much content as you can from every core asset or you will constantly be struggling to keep up with content creation demands. Nailing down your hero content can help you do both of these things.

There is no right or wrong format for building your hero content. Ebooks are often a great asset to start with because they force you to thoroughly develop your thoughts around a given topic and deliver them in a well-written, polished format. They are also a great lead magnet that prospects can download.

However, your hero content could be built out into a massive slide deck or it could start with an article. Whatever you choose, make sure that your hero content is large enough to support the creation of smaller deliverables and is the go-to source for the topic you are exploring.

Later in this book, we'll review various tactical execution options that you could employ to distribute your content.

How this applied to Readmissions Analytics

In the last chapter, I defined the content goals for the Readmissions Analytics campaign:

• Begin a relationship with personas related to quality initiatives who could champion our offering within hospitals.

• Cement our unique thought leadership position and establish our authority in the readmissions space.

• Familiarize healthcare professionals with the data required to properly analyze readmissions.

• Evangelize the true cost of readmissions so healthcare professionals could understand the financial implications of reducing readmissions.

These goals were transformed into a few themes that we explored in depth with our campaign. We began the exploration of each theme with the creation of a major piece of hero content that anchored our messaging to a key deliverable.

Theme 1 - The True Cost of Readmissions

It was extremely important to help hospital financial professionals to understand that, over the long run, it would be more expensive to pay readmissions penalties than it would be to pay the Medicare fine and accept the additional revenue associated with readmitted patients.

Hero Content - Article

This particular theme was established very early on in the product development process. The content creation process actually began by submitting an abstract to the leading publication in the hospital finance space to gauge their interest for an article dealing with this topic.

Once accepted, our leadership undertook the research and writing of a comprehensive, analytical article that demonstrated that readmissions penalties would actually cost hospitals more revenue than they would earn from excess readmissions. This article formed the basis of the hero content for this theme.

Theme 2 - Readmissions Reduction Strategies

This theme demonstrated our prowess in helping hospitals deal with the readmissions problem. The content explored various approaches for reducing readmissions at hospitals. It was intended to establish our thought leadership around the subject and to position our experts for follow-on services related to the core analytics product. It also served as an excellent introduction to personas we needed to reach outside of hospital finance, such as clinical and quality teams.

Hero Content - Ebook

The content for this theme was delivered in an ebook. This format allowed us to fully explore the subject in depth and it provided a deliverable that could serve as a lead magnet on our website. This also gave us plenty of content that we could divide and distribute through multiple other content types.

Theme 3 - How To Apply Data To Reduce Readmissions

This theme was specifically chosen to familiarize our audiences with the data available from CMS to evaluate readmissions.

Hero Content - Ebook

As with the previous theme, we chose to explore this theme in the format of an ebook first, so that we had an extensive asset that we could draw on to create other deliverables.

Acquire content from internal contributors

Unless you're the subject matter expert and the marketer too, chances are you'll be seeking contributions from other internal experts to form the nucleus of your content.

Depending on how far along your organization is on the content marketing adoption continuum, you may experience differing levels of enthusiasm among staff when it comes to helping you create content.

At the very early stages, people often can't envision why they would need to take time from their day jobs to help create what they consider marketing deliverables. If you're an experienced content marketer, this can be frustrating because you probably have a vision for your campaign and already possess an appreciation for the positive impact that content marketing can have on a business.

The key here, as with many things, is taking the time to explain why. You need to tell a vivid story so that others can understand what you're trying to do and how their contributions are essential for the success of the campaign, and ultimately, the bottom line of the business. If they believe what they are doing is important and provides them with an opportunity for recognition, you may find a more willing group of contributors. Usually, you'll be able to zero in on a champion or two who will be the first to get on board. Once they begin producing, others often join in to keep from being left behind.

Despite this, you may find that some people will still hesitate to get involved. They will say they are too busy. They will say they are looking things over. They will dodge you.

But the real reason they hesitate is simply fear.

We all fear negative criticism in one respect or another. If you're not used to publishing your work and dealing with feedback, the thought of attaching your name to something can be daunting. This is true even if they are just one of many unnamed contributors to an initiative. Someone internally will know they were a part of it and the same fear instinct kicks in. This seems counterintuitive since you're asking people to help you with something they are supposed to be an expert in. But that doesn't always get them past the trepidation of putting themselves out there.

If you're just getting the ball rolling when it comes to content marketing, the first thing you need to do is identify those early champions who want to contribute. Then you can leverage their contributions to get some quick wins that will convince others it's worth doing. Success is contagious.

When you're working with expert contributors, it's helpful to understand the strengths they bring to the table beyond their subject area knowledge. For instance, some people are excellent writers while others can barely string a paragraph together. If you're dealing with a so-so writer who can get all of the facts on the table and doesn't mind having their work heavily edited, you might find a good synergy. Other people are very sensitive about having their words moved around, so asking them to write for you may lead to unnecessary friction.

Often, subject matter experts are very busy people and can be hard to pin down. If this sounds like your situation, then you may have to get creative about how you gather content from them.

Here are a few strategies I've used to derive content from subject matter experts:

Get them writing.

Ok, not a particularly novel approach for the first suggestion, but bear with me. If you're creating content that requires deliverables such as blog posts or white papers, eventually you'll need to get the content into written form.

Sometimes, you can't judge what someone is capable of until you see what they've written. If you find a cooperative contributor, work with them to define a topic or an outline and ask them to write whatever you've agreed to. Then, see what they deliver. From there, you can figure out if what they gave you is gold, garbage, or something in between. Adjust your approach next time, based on the results from the initial go-around.

Needless to say, if they gave you garbage, you'll have to democratically suggest the necessary edits to get the final product where you need it to be.

Write something yourself and ask them to react to it.

If you have some initial content or ideas to go on, you might find that writing something yourself and asking your subject matter expert to react to it will be a more expeditious way to get the content you need.

As I mentioned earlier, some brilliant experts are so busy they can't figure out where to get started. Or maybe they are harboring some type of insecurity that is holding them back. Offering them an initial draft of something can give them a tangible place to start. This approach can work particularly well for experts who are higher up the food chain and used to directing or editing the work of others.

If you're in a highly technical industry or don't have baseline material to draw from, this technique may not be realistic. Thus, you can jump to the next strategy...

Interview them.

The thing with subject matter experts is that they usually can speak for a long time on their topics once they get going. However, not all of them are particularly talented at translating this into the written word.

If your final deliverable is something that requires a written product, you could choose to hold a recorded interview with your subject matter expert. Develop a series of questions in advance and let them unleash their knowledge into a microphone. You can then get this transcribed or simply pull the content you need from the recording to develop whatever type of written end product you require. Then, you can ask them to react to what you've created and hopefully wrap up the process quickly.

In some cases, your final product may actually be a podcast or a video, in which case your subject matter expert may never have to review a written deliverable.

You should keep one thing in mind. Some people, no matter how experienced or knowledgeable, will freeze like a deer in headlights when a microphone or camera is put in front of them. I've witnessed otherwise talkative, gregarious individuals shutting down and reverting back to reading from written notes during an interview. This might actually be fine if all you are doing is transcribing what they are saying for a blog post. But it can make for a pretty flat podcast. Again, get to know the strengths of your experts and get them doing what they do best.

Perhaps the last thing I'll leave you with should have been the first thing I said. And that is, your leadership team must be behind you for this to work. Your experts need to know that management views what you are doing with urgency and importance, or many of them will choose to find other things to spend their time on. Only when they understand the importance of your initiative to the business and see the enthusiasm from management for it will they give of their valuable time and talents. That's really only fair.

How this applied to Readmissions Analytics

By the time we started the Readmissions Analytics campaign, we already had some white papers under our belt for other business lines and an active corporate blog. While we weren't starting from the ground up in terms of content marketing at the corporate level, the notion of creating ebooks and podcasts to support the marketing of a product line was still somewhat new for the service line group with which I was working.

When I first presented my twelve month plan, they couldn't quite get their minds around how I would actually use ebook content to create several other assets or possibly why we needed an ebook in the first place. I had to explain my vision in depth, as well as what I thought the expected outcome would be.

I was lucky in the sense that they signed on quickly to the program. As we moved forward, I developed a relationship with the person who would become our main content contributor. She worked hard writing content for our first ebook, still not sure how everything would play out. However, once the ebook was published and tangible leads began to form they quickly developed an appreciation for the value of what we were doing.

From there, they were genuinely enthusiastic about creating content for each subsequent deliverable and became by far the most prolific content creators at the firm.

Select your tactical strategy

Your tactical content strategy should only emerge after you've articulated your business goals and are crystal clear on the audience(s) you plan to reach.

Surprisingly often, people undertake content creation without doing either of these things. They might say they need to create a white paper without understanding what a white paper actually is, or why it will support their strategic goals. They might start writing blog posts about random topics that may or may not support their mission.

But you are not going to be in this group because you know your goals and your audience, right?

Good. Let's start talking about tactics then.

Where to begin? There is almost an endless number of tactics you can employ when it comes to content marketing. Generally speaking, you have to plan to play the long game. It takes time for blog posts to catch on and email lists to build.

But let's face it, lead generation is the ultimate end game. In the *B2B Content Marketing 2016: Benchmarks, Budgets, and Trends – North America,* produced by *Content Marketing Institute and MarketingProfs,* 85% of marketers surveyed said lead generation is their most important content marketing goal.

Eventually your content marketing has to contribute to your

business in a tangible, measurable way - preferably related revenue and not just engagement. Over the long term, the valuable lists that you assemble should comprise the core group of people you can engage when it comes time to sell something. These lists will grow from content marketing efforts.

As you look at individual campaign assets, make sure to include specific calls-to-action that invite additional engagement. This could be as simple as adding a website address to the end of a video that someone can visit for more information.

It's probable that you'll have different kinds of assets in your campaign that will deliver different levels of value. For instance, you'll probably choose to leave your blog posts open for the public to consume. This doesn't mean they are low value, but you can use them to attract people and invite them to download a higher value asset, like a white paper, which would require them to complete a form. As you plan your campaign, map out which assets are intended to be open and which will be gated. Then you can choose the proper sequence to stage them.

Personally, I look at content marketing as an overarching umbrella that essentially means you are using content to engage your desired audience. Terms like inbound marketing and account-based marketing refer to the instruments, or approaches, you'll use to deliver your content.

First, I think it helps to start by asking what tools you have at your disposal. Do you have....?

- A website

- A blog

- A marketing automation suite

- A customer email list

- A prospect email list

- Active social media channels

- Relevant trade groups

- Third-party publishers who reach your target market

- Internal staff and/or vendors who can execute

- A known brand relevant to your targets

- Content contributors/experts

These are all things that will carry your content to your target audience or help you produce it. You don't have to have them all to begin content marketing. The important thing is to start where you are and understand what you are lacking. Plan to build up around what you do have.

You might have zero audience. No email list. No social media following. That's ok. Just realize that it could take several months for your content marketing to really gain momentum. This can be bolstered somewhat by partnering with third parties and influencers in the space, but it will still take time.

Later in this book, we'll talk about how to promote your

content through various channels. Promotion will be critical. But at this stage, you must ensure that you have a platform and network in place to create, stage, and deliver your content.

Needless to say, you should have a website of your own to serve as home base. At the very least, you can create a hub there that can deliver blog posts, Slideshare decks, videos, reports, etc.

Next, you'll want to have a way to manage email lists and deliver emails en masse to your audience. This should be the function of your marketing automation tool or set of tools, depending on your needs.

These two things are probably the minimum items you'll want to establish if you don't have them already.

At this point, it helps to look inward to evaluate the human resources and expertise you can apply towards your content program. This is huge. Don't underestimate what it will take to create content for your campaign. Sure, you can outsource some of it if you have to. But your audience really needs to hear from your people about what they know and can provide. It adds a more authentic voice to your content and will not require you to invest additional dollars in content creation when you may not have money to burn.

Some people are great speakers. Some are great writers. Some see the value in content marketing. Some could care less about marketing at all. Identify who has the knowledge to contribute to your campaign and who is willing to put forth the effort it will take to make it successful. They are not necessarily the same people.

Figure out who your champions are, so you can consider the best content approaches to make their information shine.

Additionally, before you begin to create content, you'll need to know who can create it. Will you be doing the majority of the writing? Do you have internal or external graphics support? What about audio or video? Whatever your core or extended team looks like, make sure you plan to get the talent around you that you need. I'm not saying you that you should go on a hiring binge. Depending on the scale of your program and organization, you may be able to accomplish a lot leveraging strategic external resources. I will give you specific examples of how I did this as I describe each of the tactical approaches from the Readmissions Analytics campaign.

Now comes the selection of your content types. Your job here is to align your resources so your message can then deliver that output in the most compelling vehicles you can. Additionally, you need to select content types that also align with your strategic and tactical goals so you can achieve them.

Here's what I mean.

I like blog posts. They are a great way to expand on complex topics, build an audience, maintain intimacy with that audience, and attain new traffic from search engines. They are not the best way to deliver product-related content or generate leads quickly.

Does this mean you shouldn't do blog posts if you're hyper-focused on demand generation? Of course not. But you should be realistic about where they fit into your overall content scheme so you can evaluate their performance properly. And you should plan to supplement them with content that can assist further down the funnel, so you can attempt to convert suspects into prospects more quickly.

At this point, you need to step back and look at the entire customer journey to decide what you need at each stage or step. Some people may not know you at all and may require high-level educational content to become attracted to your organization and get familiar with it. Other people, such as existing customers, may be more tolerant and even appreciative of a direct approach for your new service.

How this applied to Readmissions Analytics

Creating awareness of the readmissions problem and our product were both important. But awareness was not enough. We needed to build a list of suspects that we could qualify, so our sales team could engage with the right people.

This meant we needed to build multiple types of assets that could both attract them to us and entice them to trade their contact information for an asset.

We were fortunate that we had an existing list of contacts, a website with a blog, active social media channels, and a marketing automation platform all in place before we started. From an infrastructure standpoint, we had the tools we needed to implement a campaign.

Overall, our experts were generally willing to do public speaking and webinars as needed. Some felt more comfortable writing than others. And of course, we had to manage different styles from writer to writer. Clinical professionals are trained to write differently than people with business training. No matter what, all of our written content had to be delivered in a way that was approachable, consistent, and appropriate for our target audiences.

We did not have a graphic artist, copywriter, editor, webmaster, or video producer on our internal staff to support the launch. We filled these gaps with firms and freelancers to supplement what we could do internally. I'll discuss the specific details in each tactical section coming up.

When it came to selecting content types, there were a few criteria:

1. There had to be significant written material to support both blog posts and ebooks that could serve as lead magnets.

2. Whenever possible, our experts needed to be front and center so our target audience could get familiar with them and comfortable with our expertise.

3. We had to be able to deliver the content through our existing channels and with a minimum of technical know-

how.

4. Most of the content needed to remain relevant for a long period of time.

With all of this in mind, we proceeded to select the content types that would fit these criteria. As I mentioned previously, we developed hero content in the form of two ebooks and an article. From there, we cascaded the hero content across all of the tactical deliverables, ensuring our message stayed on point and was available to our targets in a variety of formats.

In the following sections, I will walk you through the specific content types selected, explain the benefits we saw in each one, and give you specific information on how we created them.

Tactical Approaches

Creating your specific tactical deliverables can be a lot of fun. This is when you get to see your vision truly come to life. If you've done a good job of defining your strategy, then delivering on the tactics should be a natural extension of your work.

Be realistic about the content you can create based on your timeline and resources. Plan to achieve scale from great hero content. In small and mid-size businesses particularly, you can't reinvent the wheel every time you want to create a new piece of content. Your up front investment in the hero content should pay dividends throughout your campaign.

As you work through selecting your tactical deliverables, take the time to develop a master schedule so you can see when each one should be released. This will give you a good idea as to how long you can deliver on a particular theme and if you need more content up front or other types of deliverables to round out your campaign. For instance, do you have enough deliverables that can generate demand vs. the number you have which are intended to create top-of-the-funnel awareness?

Regardless of how well you plan each piece of content, don't be afraid of serendipity. You may have great ideas along the way or opportunities may present themselves that you never considered in advance. Keep trying things and prepare to be agile.

Also, keep in mind that not every piece of content is going to perform well. As you move through a campaign, you will get a sense as to which themes your audience is responding to and which types of assets they prefer to engage with. You may have to reconsider some of your future deliverables based on what you've learned initially.

The tactical approaches I'll discuss in the following sections are the ones we focused on for the Readmissions Analytics campaign. This is not an exhaustive list of all the potential things you could do, of course. The tactics we selected worked in synergy, and represented the best methods for reaching our target audience and repurposing content so we could get the most from our content creation efforts.

Ebooks

Ebooks

Like the name implies, an ebook is an electronic book. Most typically delivered in the form of a PDF, ebooks are excellent for delivering comprehensive content.

Don't let the name fool you. An ebook does not have to be a 60,000 word novel. But they are usually more than a page or two. They can include graphics and have stunning design quality or they can be simple and filled with more text than anything else.

Why do Ebooks work?

Ebooks are high-value assets.
Because ebooks are typically educational in nature and provide deep dives on topics, they make perfect lead magnets. You can post them on your website and require individuals to fill out a form to access the ebook. Since the audience expects to gain access to a fair amount of knowledge, they are usually more willing to provide their email and other pertinent contact information for that access. The more value they perceive, the more information they may be willing to provide.

Of course, you could also offer your ebook without requiring a form to be filled out. This will really depend on what your strategy is behind the asset.

Often, the strategy behind marketing an ebook is to build an email list, so the ebook is offered for free as long as the person downloading it is willing to provide basic contact information. However, in certain circumstances, you could choose to charge a nominal fee for the ebook. This could raise the perceived value of the asset, but it could reduce the number of downloads you attract.

Further, if you go the extra mile of converting your ebook into a format for e-readers and make it available on a platform like Amazon, you will not know who actually downloaded the ebook. This will ultimately all depend on your strategy. In most typical content marketing campaigns, your ebook will be offered for free.

Ebooks can coalesce your thinking on a topic.

If you take the time to develop a comprehensive, well-written ebook, you will have an asset that can truly define your best thinking on a topic.

This is why ebooks make great cornerstone content assets. Different ebooks can cover different themes that become your go-to source of content for each subject area.

You can divide ebook content and deliver it in multiple formats.

Each ebook you write could give you a plethora of content you can use elsewhere.

For instance, you could pull sections from the ebook, and with some editing, form them into individual blog posts -

each with a call-to-action to download the original ebook. You could drip these posts out on a fixed schedule and continue exploring your key themes over time.

You could pull quotes to use as social media posts. Or you could extract key statistics, if you have them, and make infographics.

Ebook content could form the basis of podcasts, articles, webinars, live presentations and more.

Ebooks can be promoted widely.

Of course you'll do everything you can to tell your target audience about your ebook through your existing contact lists, social media channels, salespeople, etc.

You can also turn to your business partners to help you promote the ebook. What if they could include links to your download page in their newsletter, send a dedicated email blast to their list, or promote on their social networks?

If you have dollars to place behind the promotion, you could leverage third-party publishers, most of which will offer some vehicle for syndicating or promoting your ebook.

Ebooks can be printed.

Ok, it probably seems counterintuitive to say that you should print an electronic book. But in certain cases, getting your ebook formatted into a professionally formatted, nicely printed deliverable may be a great option.

Think about having your ebook on a trade show table or as something a salesperson could leave behind after a call. Depending on your unique circumstances, this could be a viable option for circulating your content more widely.

Distribution options abound.

Often, the main delivery vehicle for your ebook will be your own website. The typical arrangement is that someone visits the site, fills out a form, and is then redirected to your ebook.

However, there are other alternatives that can be effective as well. Ebooks can be loaded to Slideshare for instance. You can leave them open for public view, or you can place a lead form in front of the content, much as you would on your own website. The advantage is that Slideshare generates a tremendous amount of organic traffic which could help your ebook be discovered by people you don't already know.

As I mentioned before, if you choose to charge for your ebook, Amazon and other online book sellers could be an option for you.

Another option is to provide private links to the ebook that salespeople could use to send to key contacts, for example.

How this applied to Readmissions Analytics

Two of our three cornerstone assets were ebooks. We selected ebooks because they provided robust assets that could act as lead magnets and because they created a tremendous amount of content that could be leveraged in other formats.

The ebook content came mainly from one internal expert who created initial drafts based on outlines we developed and agreed to. Once the draft content was submitted, I read them for content, flow, and grammar, made suggestions and finalized them with the author. Then I sent the drafts to a freelance artist, who created a template for the ebooks and completed the layouts. Each ebook was about 13 pages in length.

The ebooks thoroughly explored two of our major themes. The process of creating them helped us to refine our message while carefully crafting language that spoke to our target audience.

These ebooks were available free on our website after prospects completed a form. We also posted them on Slideshare, but with no form required. Each time we released an ebook, they produced a flurry of downloads and other activity on our website, which was our primary goal.

Our intention from the beginning was to carve up the content in each ebook for use on our blog. We didn't know exactly how each ebook would be divided until they were written, but our original outlines reflected the need to break out the content into sections for this purpose.

Ultimately, several blog posts were created from ebook content or associated topics. In fact, the highest performing blog post from the entire series was written using content that was on the cutting room floor because it didn't quite fit into either of the ebooks. That's what I mean when I talked about serendipity in the last section!

Both ebooks were promoted heavily to our house email lists. One performed much better than the other, but both did well overall.

Additionally, both ebooks were promoted over LinkedIn and Twitter. Specifically, we employed LinkedIn sponsored updates to reach our target personas.

One of the ebooks was also promoted through a third-party publishing partner who hosted it on their website and marketed it to their subscriber base.

Each time someone downloaded an ebook from our website, the relevant salesperson was alerted via email and could make the choice to follow up directly depending on the profile match of the person who downloaded the ebook.

Just one last thought on ebooks - they are different than white papers. For this particular campaign, we chose the ebook format. White papers serve a slightly different function and typically have a more structured format. I say this because sometimes the terms are used somewhat interchangeably, but they are not really the same thing.

Video

Video

Video in and of itself does not require much explanation. We have all watched video at some point, whether it's a television program, dancing cats on YouTube, or a corporate explainer video.

In the context of B2B content marketing, video is not usually delivered over television. You're more likely to find recorded video on platforms like YouTube, Facebook, Vimeo, and even Slideshare. Live video is making a splash on Twitter via Periscope and Meerkat and over services like Blab.

Why do videos work?

According to the *The B2B Video Content Marketing Survey* conducted by the Web Video Marketing Council, ReelSEO and Flimp Media during Q3 of 2015, 96% of B2B organizations surveyed were engaged in video content marketing.

Why is this format so popular? Here are a few reasons that come to mind:

The volume and diversity of potential content is immeasurable.

The range of topics that can be covered in video is truly remarkable. From simple how-to videos, to testimonials, product promotion, entertainment, behind-the-scenes interviews and more, video can deliver an impressive amount of content in a short amount of time.

Video holds attention.

If you're covering something relevant, even a video with marginal production quality can be riveting.

Video is widely available.

Bandwidth constraints are no longer an issue. Anyone on a desktop or mobile device that's connected to the Internet can stream recorded or live video with good resolution.

The proliferation of video delivery platforms makes distributing your video content very easy. It's also usually free. You have to consider the context of a video you might deliver on YouTube vs. one you post on Facebook. Still, there are many options available.

Producing videos is more cost-effective than it used to be.

Anyone with a smartphone and a social media account can record and distribute video. Granted, the production value may not be Hollywood quality, but you can still get video out there that is relevant and important to your audience almost instantly.

There are all kinds of options for producing video compared to just a few years ago. Your needs, the nature of the video, and your budget will drive what you can ultimately produce, but the bar for creating video is overall much lower than it used to be. There is also a greater tolerance among audiences for video that is not extremely polished, provided the message still gets across.

How this applied to Readmissions Analytics

The initial video elements for the campaign consisted of an animated explainer video for the product and a series of live conference speaker videos.

First, we wanted to have a short video available that could frame the readmissions issue and demonstrate briefly how our product specifically could help solve the problem. It was decided that the best way to do this would be by creating an animated video that included voiceover and a music background. While I could write the script for the video, we did not have a motion animator on staff, nor did I necessarily want to bring on an agency to handle the production. So I turned to a trusted solo freelancer for the work.

Once I had an initial script available, I worked with the freelancer to create a storyboard, select the voiceover talent and the music. Then he went about creating the video itself.

The finished piece came in at under two minutes and cost a few thousand dollars to produce. Not chump change, but certainly less than it could have cost. I posted the video to YouTube, which enabled me to embed it on our website and share on social media. I also posted it on Slideshare.

As our program evolved, we decided to hold our own seminar on the topic of readmissions for one local market. It was to be a day-long program featuring several of our experts talking about specific areas of readmissions that addressed our core themes. Our experts developed sessions that were about 1/2 hour long each and were supported by PowerPoint.

To get the most out of these sessions, we decided to videotape them, creating another core set of content assets. For these videos, I felt it was important that they were professionally videotaped mainly because:

1. I wanted the videos to be well lit, in focus and free from jitters.

2. I wanted the audio to be high quality which meant having wireless microphones on the speakers.

I didn't need a multi-camera point of view, makeup, editing and other production items like that. I just needed a solidly recorded end product and digital files I could make minor edits to. For these videos, I hired a freelance videographer who owned the proper camera, lighting, and audio equipment. He set up in a single position for the day and videotaped each speaker in turn. Then he sent me the digital files a couple of days later.

The Content Driven Product Launch

Our explainer video had a nice introduction, with our logo flying in and an audio stinger. I asked the artist who created that video to send me just that four-second opening clip. Once I had that, I was able to bring that opener and the videos of the sessions into Adobe Premiere for minor editing.

I placed the opening clip at the beginning of the timeline, of course, and then inserted a speaker video. Throughout each video, I spliced in certain PowerPoint slides from the original presentation, so that viewers could easily see what was on screen, in the event the speaker referred to something not visible on the original video. I also cut out any segments where there were long pauses, mistakes, etc.

We ended up with three finished videos that ran about 1/2 hour each. They were exported into MP4 files and loaded to YouTube. From there, each video was embedded on our website and shared on social media.

These videos delivered very in-depth content and made excellent companion assets to our ebooks and other content deliverables.

Our video content performed reasonably well in terms of engagement compared to other assets in the campaign. At a minimum, the conference recordings enhanced our image and developed our brand by introducing our internal experts to many prospects and industry professionals.

The explainer video was used extensively by our sales team during prospecting efforts, in addition to promotion we did through our marketing initiatives.

Articles

Articles

For the most part, articles are meant to be non-promotional examinations of topics that educate and inform audiences.

Everyone is familiar with articles, whether they are business oriented or for any number of topics. Articles can be delivered online, through e-newsletters, and even still in print!

The thing is, not everyone thinks of articles as a way to promote themselves and their business. Here are some reasons why you should.

Why do articles work?

Articles are a powerful tactic in the content marketing toolkit. Done well, they give you the opportunity to explore a topic in depth and demonstrate your mastery of it.

Distribution Potential.

While self-publishing is certainly a viable option, focused third-party publications can showcase your expertise to a wider range of your target market than you might be able to reach on your own. These publications often have a critical mass of devoted readers who trust the content they publish and look forward to receiving it.

Authority.

Articles published by respected third parties can add an element of authenticity, legitimacy and authority to your initiative in ways that other media just can't. People expect that leading publications maintain a level of editorial control ensuring that only the most relevant, well-written content is circulated.

Range of Publishing Options.

These days, there are a range of publishing options available to help you distribute articles that you author. Of course, the fastest and simplest way is to publish your own content to your blog or proprietary newsletter. Alternatively, LinkedIn offers a platform called *Pulse*, which enables anyone with an account to publish an article. This can help bolster views of your content and contribute to it being shared over the social network and beyond.

While self-publishing is very common, it often helps to publish with sources beyond your immediate control to enhance your potential distribution.

There are different ways to approach publishing with other sources.

In certain circumstances, a guest post on an industry-focused blog or newsletter may be desirable. If you have identified a key publication that accepts contributions, you may be able to submit your article to them for distribution or pitch them on an idea. The key here is that the other party is selecting only the best articles to publish, giving your article an instant level of gravitas.

Another approach is to write for a community-contributed website such as *Business 2 Community*. In this instance, authors are screened initially to ensure that the quality of their work is at a reasonable level. Once approved, the author is given access to a page where they can write and stage their article for approval. As in the previous example, there is no guarantee that your article will be accepted for publication. But, if you follow their guidelines and craft your article so it is relevant to their readers, you stand a pretty good chance of getting published reasonably fast.

There are other contributed sources such as *The Huffington Post* or *Forbes,* which are more general in nature. These publications are stringent about the contributions they publish and may require that you are first accepted into their contributor network, which is a higher bar to surmount than some other sites. It can be worthwhile to write for these sites because they receive massive traffic. However, they are probably better if you work in an industry vertical that enables you to write on topics with mass appeal as opposed to a very technical niche, for instance.

The top flight of third party publishing is for major industry trade journals or similar publications. Often, writing for these sources will require you to submit an article abstract describing the intention of your article and identifying the contributing writers. This abstract is typically vetted by an editorial board who selects only the top tier of ideas. Then, your draft article may be subject to peer review and editing before it is finally published online or in print.

As you can imagine, this process can take several months. However, because of the care they take in selecting and preparing the articles, these publications can lend significant credence to you and your topic. They are also usually laser-focused on a specific target market, putting your content directly in front of those you need to see it most.

How this applied to Readmissions Analytics

Before we had a product to sell or a marketing campaign planned, our leadership team knew that we needed to lay a foundation in the market that demonstrated our expertise around the readmissions topic.

Because the issue was so new and many hospital leaders had misconceptions about the nature of the Medicare program, we decided to deal with these concerns head-on in the form of an article. Optimally, the best place for this article to appear was the leading trade publication for hospital financial professionals. The concept began with an abstract that we submitted for review to their editorial board. We were fortunate they had interest in the topic and agreed to accept an article from us.

Our authors set about performing an extensive data analysis to back up the assertions we planned to make. Then they crafted the article and sent it in for peer review.

After several months, we received edits back and then a few months after that, the article ran in their print and online editions under the title, *The True Financial Impact of Hospital Readmissions*. Needless to say, this put our firm front and center as a thought leader for a burning issue among our exact target audience. It was a huge score.

Beyond the thousands of print and online readers exposed to the article directly, we also commissioned reprints for use by our sales team at customer meetings and exhibitions. A PDF of the article was loaded to our Slideshare page and then embedded on our website as a resource for visitors.

As one would hope, the exposure that the article provided gave way to inquiries for speaking engagements, webinars, and article-writing opportunities for other publications. Additionally, the authority it gave us set the stage for subsequent deliverables later issued as part of our content marketing campaign.

In addition to this major national article, we also created smaller, off-the-shelf articles that chapters of the national organization could run in their regional newsletters. Topics usually dealt with sub-issues related to the readmissions program. These articles helped us to reach hospital financial professionals at the grassroots level.

Speaking Engagements

Speaking Engagements

In the context of B2B marketing, most live speaking engagements tend to be for trade groups, conferences, or at other educational events like seminars or classes.

Speaking engagements can run the gamut from small, intimate events to large-scale meetings with thousands of attendees.

Some speaking engagements are paid. However, many are not, especially if you're a vendor within an industry. However, if you're trying to build awareness of your subject or even your offering, there are few better options for evangelizing it to a captive audience of dozens, hundreds, or even thousands of people.

Why do speaking engagements work?

They give you credibility and authority.

Like third-party published articles, speaking at an event gives you and your message an air of legitimacy and authority that is hard to attain otherwise. You are on a stage, literally or figuratively, because the organizers of an event have deemed you to be an expert in your craft or on a topic. They go to great lengths to promote your presence as part of their event and lend their credibility to you as part of that exchange.

They build your reputation.

If you want to be recognized as a thought leader, then live speaking is an important part of building your reputation. As an audience listens and engages with you, they begin to see you as a go-to source in your field. This can lead to additional speaking or writing opportunities and even to business inquiries as they see you, or your firm, as someone who can help them to solve their problems. That's the whole point of content marketing, right!

They provide exposure.

Once you are part of a conference agenda or selected as an instructor, for instance, the organizers of that initiative will typically include your subject and bio as part of the marketing for whatever type of event or class they are promoting. This promotion gives you and your firm exposure before you even step on stage.

Once you're there live, your message will be delivered to any number of attendees. You will have their attention for as long as your time slot allows. That intimate level of contact is hard to replicate.

They can help you get campaign content.

Sometimes, thought leaders within an organization can be

difficult to pin down when it comes to writing blog posts or papers, for instance. However, many recognize the value of being a featured speaker at an event. It gives them direct contact with their peer network and keeps them in front of the "right" people.

If these thought leaders are inclined to pursue their own speaking engagements, they are typically very committed to creating slides or other material necessary for their presentation. Many will also create speaker notes or bullets to help guide their talk.

This material can be a goldmine for you as a content creator. Perhaps you can ask your expert to record the session afterwards using some type of screen capture software. Or maybe they will allow you to repurpose their notes into a blog post or other deliverable. Maybe their slides would be suitable for posting on Slideshare. Take their lead and leverage what they are most comfortable doing to your advantage.

How this applied to Readmissions Analytics

Speaking engagements gave our experts the opportunity to explore the readmissions issue in depth with audiences all over the United States. Our main topic mirrored our national article, *The True Financial Impact of Hospital Readmissions*. This allowed us to take the message of the article and amplify it live to audiences throughout the year.

The process began, as most do, by submitting abstracts to regional and national organizations pitching our topic. Fortunately, our topic was very timely and of concern to our target audience, so we were able to land several important speaking engagements. We didn't get them all by far, but we did well, even landing one major national conference.

The majority of our speaking engagements were to regional chapters for the national hospital finance association that published our article. These gatherings typically drew anywhere from 20-50 people per session - sometimes more, sometimes less.

We were able to videotape at least one of these events, which we posted to YouTube and embedded on our website.

As I mentioned back in the section on video, we also decided to hold a day-long seminar where several of our speakers could explore multiple facets of the readmissions issue. Recruiting for this event turned out to be difficult, although we ended up with enough registrations to hold it.

It didn't help that it snowed just enough the morning of the event to keep some people from traveling in for it.

Needless to say, attendance did not overwhelm us. However, we did manage to generate ninety minutes of finished, edited video from the event which we used as part of the campaign. You have to turn lemons into lemonade whenever you can!

Podcasts

Podcasts

Podcasts are audio recordings that can be streamed or downloaded via websites or services like iTunes.

Podcasts can take on many formats, from interview-style shows with multiple people participating, analogous to a talk radio program, to a single individual discussing an idea. Podcasts come in various lengths from just a couple of minutes to an hour or more.

Creating a podcast is not extremely difficult, but it takes quite a bit of preparation, along with the right equipment and process to do it correctly.

Why do podcasts work?

Podcasting still has open space.
Let's face it, there is a lot of content out there these days. B2B buyers are deluged with offers to download papers, participate in webinars, and visit blogs, and their inboxes are filled daily with e-newsletters of all kinds.

While there are literally thousands of podcasts available, the podcasting space is still considered an underutilized medium. This is particularly true if you plan to podcast on a niche topic to a targeted audience. It's conceivable you'll find that no one else is there producing the kind of content you can contribute.

Podcasts generate engagement.

There are few other content tactics where an individual will take the time to explore your topic for more than a few minutes.

But with podcasting, you can capture a listener's attention for much longer periods of time. Consider a podcast that is fifteen minutes long, a half hour, or even an hour! You'll have a listener's devoted attention for that entire time.

This creates a level of familiarity and trust that few other tactics can offer.

Podcasts are widely accessible.

Podcasts are more accessible than ever and the rate of adoption continues to climb.

Podcasts are generally hosted on a website, so that a feed is available for outside podcast applications to read. Regular visitors to your website could choose to listen to your program through a built-in media player if you choose.

However, the real power of podcasting is that your show can be available on most mobile devices. If you submit your podcast to iTunes, the world's most powerful podcast search engine, your podcast becomes available to millions of people who have Apple phones and tablets.

The Content Driven Product Launch

With the advent of Apple CarPlay, people can access your podcast right through their vehicle's dashboard. Apple also offers a podcast app on their Apple TV device. Unlike other media, people can consume your podcast content while they are working out, driving, or just relaxing.

Android devices have several different types of apps that can play podcasts, so you can make your feed available to them as well.

There are also other services such as Stitcher and SoundCloud that can deliver podcasts. They have their own apps and many people find them to be a viable alternative for getting podcast content.

You can explore topics in-depth.

Podcasts offer you the ability to dive deep into topics in an entertaining and informative format. Sometimes, hearing an expert explain a difficult concept can make it much more approachable than having to read a lengthy paper, for instance.

Many podcasters focus on very specific items in each episode so you know exactly what you'll learn with time you invest.

You can build an audience.

The main goal of content marketers is to build an audience that can eventually become the nucleus of a paying customer base. If you maintain a consistent publishing schedule, inform and entertain, you stand a good chance of building a loyal audience that comes back regularly to hear the insights you offer.

Podcasts are not generally a "one and done". They are a medium that you commit to, in order to serve your target audience. After delivering value through time you earn the right to ask for their business without being overly promotional or aggressive.

You create content that you can repurpose.

One of the easiest things you can do with podcast content is to have the audio transcribed. There are many services that can do this inexpensively from the audio file you supply them. By doing this, you instantly acquire written content that you can use to form the basis of blog posts, ebooks, and so on.

Moreover, this content is almost always keyword rich, especially if you are focusing on a specific topic. The benefit is that the keywords are built into the conversation as opposed to being strategically, and sometimes awkwardly placed into an article. Generally speaking, this should have a positive effect on SEO if you use the transcript on a blog.

These transcripts also tend to be long form, which is helpful if you have trouble writing long articles or little time to do so. A twenty-minute podcast could easily translate into a transcript in excess of 2,500 words.

How this applied to Readmissions Analytics

At BESLER, we did not have a regular podcast, but we saw utility in the format. There were few, if any, firms delivering the unique information we could offer to the audience we wanted to attract through podcasts.

We decided to create a special, six-part podcast series to support the launch of Readmissions Analytics. This was not intended to be an ongoing show, but we did consider the possibility of creating a regular program if these episodes were successful.

To form the basis of the shows, we selected six sections from the ebooks we previously issued. The interview-style podcasts explored each topic with a leading clinician who was a former chief medical officer at a hospital. He discussed readmissions reduction strategies, financial impacts, and data available for analysis. This worked because he was able to offer C-suite perspectives on how the readmissions problem was viewed and he was able to speak to the topics from both a clinical and financial perspective, helping us to appeal to the key audiences we needed to address.

We dripped out each audio episode on our blog over a six-week period. The program was also available on iTunes and SoundCloud.

All of the audio content was transcribed and then formatted into separate blog posts that we published long after the initial audio versions were available. This gave us a two-for-one benefit for each episode. All of the posts contained a call to action back to one of the ebooks, so that we could drive downloads and produce tangible leads.

From a production perspective, we did not make a major technology investment to produce these programs. We literally purchased two USB microphones and I recorded the audio on my laptop using Adobe Premiere. This was not an optimal approach, but it produced a reasonable end product. I added some license-free music and voiceover to create show bumpers, leveled the audio a bit, and then exported MP3s.

Our website is on Wordpress, which gave me some options for delivering the audio. After some research, I settled on the PowerPress plug-in and hosted our audio files on Blubrry, the media hosting service which makes PowerPress. This proved to be a good decision as PowerPress integrates very well with WordPress and the service fees for hosting were extremely reasonable.

After a few episodes were available on our blog, I submitted the podcast feed to iTunes for indexing on their directory. The approval process was very swift and we were up on iTunes within a couple of days.

I also started a free SoundCloud account and posted our audio files there. This is a good choice if you plan to promote the podcasts on social media, as their player looks excellent on platforms like LinkedIn and Twitter and allows users to listen to the audio directly from those platforms.

Bear in mind that there is some additional setup required if you want your podcast to appear correctly. You'll need to do things like add cover art and configure the ID3 tags on each MP3 file. There are some detailed, paid podcasting courses out there which cover everything from setup to promotion. In my case, I was able to get a great education on the subject for free through many of the websites and YouTube videos available on the subject.

I'm happy to say that, based on the success of these initial programs, we decided to produce a weekly podcast series covering a wider range of hospital financial topics. For this new show, we made a more extensive investment in equipment so the recordings sounded much better than the original readmissions series. I switched to Audacity for recording and editing the episodes, which is robust enough to handle our needs and is absolutely free. For about $60, I had professional talent from Voice Bunny record the show opening and closing, adding a much more polished feel to the end product.

Webinars

Webinars

Webinars are typically live events consisting of audio and video, often a slide presentation, conducted over the Internet and accessible via a web browser or mobile application.

Webinars can require some form of pre-registration or they can be freely accessible to anyone with a web link to the webinar.

The webinar format is used for anything from education to product demonstrations. In the context of content marketing, webinars typically have an educational component followed by a call-to-action for attendees.

Why do webinars work?

They're the next best thing to being there.

Webinars allow attendees from several geographic locations to gather virtually to listen to a live presentation. They have similar benefits to live speaking engagements in that a thought leader can share knowledge on a topic they are expert in, interact with the audience, and demonstrate their competence.

The audience can consume this content live and enjoy the

experience from wherever they happen to be.

The audience can participate.
Often times, webinar presenters encourage participation from attendees through live polling or chat. This allows the audience to direct feedback to presenters, and ask questions of experts to whom they would otherwise not have access. This makes the experience more fruitful and memorable long after the event.

You can ask for them to act.
It is not atypical for a webinar host to encourage some type of action during a webinar, even those with an educational focus. Audiences are astute and by seeing who the sponsors of the webinar are, they can glean what they will probably be pitched.

The worst webinars are when a host organization reels in attendees by promising them one thing, then spends the entire time doing a demo of their product. This will turn an audience off. As a host, if you've done a good job of articulating a problem and advanced a potential solution which leads someone to logically consider your offering, then asking attendees to take a next step with you is perfectly acceptable.

You can measure engagement.
Many webinar applications will allow you to see when

people enter and exit your webinar. Some will even help you understand if people are doing other things on their computer when you expect them to be participating.

You can also view engagement based on the quantity and types of questions you receive, and registrations versus actual attendees.

You can follow up.

If you require a registration in order for someone to attend, you've developed a valuable list of people interested in a topic. Based on whether they attend or not, you can decide how best to follow up with them.

Webinar audiences are often highly engaged potential prospects who are excellent candidates for follow-up after the actual session.

You get a recording.

Webinar applications typically allow you to record sessions. You can use this recording in a number of different ways, depending on the nature of the content.

At a minimum, you may wish to make it available to registrants. For those who attended, it is a valuable reference and for those who did not, it allows them to view the webinar on demand.

In certain cases, you may wish to make the webinar more publicly available on your website or on YouTube, for example. You can then promote it just as you would any other asset, even asking for a form to be filled out before viewing it.

Another option is to transcribe the session and use that content similar to what I suggested in the Podcast section earlier.

How this applied to Readmissions Analytics

We participated in two kinds of webinars to discuss readmissions - those we hosted and those hosted by other organizations.

For webinars that we hosted, we stayed focused on our message by essentially presenting the same information we covered in our speaking engagements around the true financial impact of readmissions. This enabled us to create one core set of slides that we could use (with minor alterations) in various formats.

Pre-registration was mandatory for our webinars and we marketed them heavily to our proprietary contact list, and occasionally, through third parties. Our webinars were held using Go-To-Meeting, with a single expert presenter walking through a series of slides.

One thing that did make our webinars unique, and actually helped with the marketing, is that BESLER is an approved provider of CPE credit. For CPAs who desired continuing education, attending our webinar would help them earn that credit. This meant a couple of things for us. First, we could not be at all promotional with our content. We could point people to additional resources, which we did, but that was all. Second, we had to run polls through the webinar to ensure the audience maintained engagement and we could prove that, if audited.

One thing to remember is that with all live events, you have to expect the unexpected. Technical glitches can occur. People may have trouble connecting and try calling in for support. You have to be ready to handle any number of contingencies that could arise. Doing a dry run of your webinar is always a good idea if you can gather everyone in advance. Sometimes it's just less stressful to engage a company that runs webinars professionally to handle the registration and the logistics of the live presentation. This can be especially helpful if your audience is large.

As you might expect, we followed up with webinar attendees by offering them access to the recorded version and other resources from our content arsenal. Our salespeople were provided with a list of registrants, indicating their attendance status, so they could follow up accordingly.

We were fortunate in that many of the regional hospital financial organizations we worked with were looking for webinar content that they could offer to their members as a way to keep them engaged with their chapters. Working in concert with them on promotion and logistics, we presented this same readmissions content to their members as part of chapter educational initiatives.

This was great practice for live speaking engagements and it enabled us to reach many of the same people without having to travel as often. The downside is that the organizations usually would not release the names of attendees to us, so we had to rely on them approaching us for more information after the fact, as opposed to our own proactive follow-up.

Blogs

Blogs

A Google search of the word "blog" delivers the following definition:

A regularly updated website or web page, typically one run by an individual or small group, that is written in an informal or conversational style.

Typically, blog posts appear in chronological order and can be grouped into categories so users can review posts dealing with the same topic.

Why do blogs work?

They build an audience.

Perhaps the single biggest reason that businesses blog is to build an audience. By delivering consistent, helpful content, businesses can develop loyal followers who are much more likely to convert when they do ask for a sale.

Because of your blog, these followers will have a reason to visit your website again and again, strengthening your relationship and building trust.

They attract new prospects.
Well-written, optimized blog posts stand a better than average chance of attaining a good rank on Google and other search engines for the topics they address.

This organic traffic from search engines can deliver new readers to your website who may go on to subscribe to your blog, download content assets, or even inquire about your product or service.

They leverage multiple content formats.
While blog content is usually driven by text, it is easy to embed video, audio, and Slideshare files, for example.

They can be shared and they link to content.
Blog posts are easily shared on social media or through email. Moreover, you can add additional value to posts and enhance your SEO by linking to relevant outside resources.

It also works the other way, as potential customers and others in your industry share your content and link back to your posts from their websites, creating referral traffic.

They establish thought leadership.
As you begin to help your audience solve their issues through your blog posts, you become an authoritative source of information for them. You can elevate your company from being "just another vendor" to a valuable resource worthy of attention among your industry peers

and prospects alike.

How this applied to Readmissions Analytics

Since our blog really was the glue that tied many tactics together, this is best explained as the last item in our sequence of tactics.

Here is a recap of how we repurposed content on our blog from existing assets:

Ebooks

Earlier on, I talked about how our ebooks were divided so that sections of them could be turned into standalone blog posts. This provided for excellent foundational content on our blog that could be prepared and scheduled to trickle out over time. Each individual post advertised the full ebooks so that we could continue to drive downloads far after their initial publication.

Podcasts

Transcripts of each podcast were converted into full blog posts. These were long posts, filled with important keywords used naturally in the context of a conversation. The podcast posts linked back to the pages containing the podcast audio.

Video

Videos taken of our experts from live conferences were embedded into blog posts from YouTube. We included a short description of the video content along with the embedded material. These videos ran about 1/2 hour each and dove deep into specific topics related to our core themes.

Slideshare

Embedded articles and worksheets from Slideshare were included on related posts to further enhance the content on those posts.

Beyond repurposed content, we also created original posts that dealt with timely issues, such as the issuance of new data from CMS or vital statistics. These types of posts often did very well because of their specificity and relevance to our niche market.

Back in the section relating to ebooks, I referenced an instance where a blog created from content that hit the cutting room floor turned into the best blog post of the campaign. Let me elaborate on that for you so you can see the power of serendipity!

One week in late March of 2015, I was looking over our blog schedule and I wanted to fill a gap in April with something related to readmissions content (our corporate blog handles many other topics related to hospital finance). As I had already written and scheduled many posts from our previous ebook and video content, I was looking for something a bit different to shake up the rhythm.

I started looking through manuscripts of our papers, speaker notes, articles - really anything I could get my hands on for ideas. I came across a manuscript from one of our ebooks that contained a significant redline. In fact, we had decided to pull out an entire section. This section dealt with how to calculate the LACE risk score, which is essentially a method for screening patients at a hospital to determine their likelihood to readmit.

I knew that at a seminar we held, one of our key speakers spent quite a bit of time reviewing this topic. We had videotaped him and used the video in another blog post. I watched the video and remembered that he had distributed to the audience a brief, one-page worksheet demonstrating how to calculate the LACE risk score.

Without a great deal of planning, I extracted the redlined copy from the manuscript and created a blog post from it. Then I loaded the one-page worksheet to Slideshare and embedded it in the blog post. Working in Wordpress, I used Yoast to optimize the page for the key term, "Lace Risk Score". Then I hit the publish button. That was early April 2015.

Not much happened right away, but by June, we started to see a significant uptick in traffic to the site. Using Google Analytics, it wasn't hard to figure out that the blog post on the LACE risk score was now driving quite a bit of traffic. As the months rolled on, this post picked up steam and eventually landed at the top of page one on Google for the search, "lace risk score". Moreover, the one-page Slideshare worksheet showed up in results on page two or three most of the time.

As of April 2016, about one year after initial publication, this post has achieved over 13,500 unique page views, which is substantial for our business niche. The Slideshare worksheet alone has been viewed around 22,000 times.

I wish I could boast that I was some type of SEO genius or that my superior content planning skills led to such an incredible result. The truth is that I just worked with what I had and tried to create something that our audience would find relevant. Of course, I used the tools at my disposal to optimize the post and did my best to properly format the blog post and the Slideshare worksheet for search engine indexing. The result has been greater than I could have possibly planned for.

There is no question that without our blog tying all of our content together, the campaign would not have had the lasting impact that we desired.

Additional approaches

The previous sections on tactical approaches covered the core content elements we used in The Readmissions Analytics campaign.

In addition to those core elements, there were a few other items worth mentioning that supported the overall effort.

Infographic

An infographic was created entitled, *Why You Should Care About The Medicare Hospital Readmissions Reduction Program*. This infographic was designed to help our audience understand the significance of the new penalty program by using a variety of statistics illustrating general readmissions trends throughout the United States and several that are specific to the program.

The infographic was housed on our Slideshare channel. We actively shared it across LinkedIn and Twitter for well over a year. We also enlarged the infographic and used it as a stand-up display at our exhibition booth in 2015.

Not long after the infographic was loaded to Slideshare, we received an inquiry from the Health Care Compliance Association with a request to use it as the infographic of the month in their national publication, *Compliance Today*. This magazine goes out monthly to 9,500 healthcare compliance professionals and institutions. While not our core target market, this group was influential in the purchasing decision for a product like ours.

Print Ad

We had a standing monthly ad placement in the national publication of the largest healthcare finance association in the country. A readmissions print ad ran for several months of the year.

The headline of the ad asked, "Is your hospital one of the 2,610 receiving reduced Medicare payments in 2015 due to excess readmissions?"

The ad went on to explain the benefits of our service and invited readers to a landing page where they could watch our explainer video.

This ad was also placed in various local chapter newsletters of the parent healthcare finance organization.

Sales activation

Our sales team was furnished with product training and several resources to help them target and engage prospects.

Each regional vice president was given a list of the top 25 targets in their territories, including the readmissions penalty for each facility, along with a template email to help their outreach.

They were provided with a sell sheet along with electronic versions of our ebooks and articles. Leveraging Hubspot, each regional vice president was delivered immediate notifications of website revisits and e-book downloads for any prospect in their territories related to readmissions.

A demo version of the offering was created accompanied by a document describing each report contained in the offering so they could explain the benefits of each respectively.

Training was held to help our sales team focus on both sharing valuable content and identifying leads on social media, primarily LinkedIn. As part of our overall employee advocacy efforts, a social sharing SaaS tool was integrated to make sharing corporate approved social media posts extremely easy for them. This kept them on message while driving valuable traffic towards key areas of our website that supported their selling efforts.

Account-based marketing

Sales were supported directly through a multi-part email nurturing campaign to select hospitals that experienced large year-over-year penalty increases or large penalties compared to their peers nationally.

These messages came under each salesperson's signature and were personalized with contact information including the unique penalty amount of each facility.

This effort generated interest from several prospects and led to the first closed sale of the product.

Penalty Calculator

A calculator was available on our website for download after a contact form was filled in. This calculator, formatted in MS Excel, allowed prospects to model future changes to their projected readmissions penalties based on various criteria.

This was a sophisticated and interesting tool, but downloads of it never came close to other assets such as our ebooks.

Promote and distribute your content

There are almost a limitless number of ways to promote content today. It would be difficult, if not impossible, for me to attempt to name or review them all here, not to mention that different situations require different promotional tactics depending on the audience, your own resources, and context.

Instead, in this section, I'll dive deep into each of the main promotional vehicles we used to promote Readmissions Analytics. All of them can be utilized in just about any B2B marketing situation.

Email

Email

By now, it probably goes without saying that an email list is one of, if not the most important assets a business can have. We all send and receive business emails each day, so this is not a novel tactic per se.

For years, the death of email has been discussed and projected. However, email still remains an important line of communication to business contacts. Even with average open rates hovering around 20% and click rates down under 4% depending on where you look, email can still have a positive impact if you focus on providing tremendous value to your audience.

Why does email work?

Email is direct.

An email inbox is a very personal thing. It's a place where direct communications are sent to you and you have a choice as to how and when you will deal with them. It's also a place where this information is aggregated, perhaps filed, and maintained for later reference or documentation.

We all receive unsolicited emails. Oftentimes, these are intrusive and we delete them immediately. But for those important messages that come from people or organizations we know and trust, emails can serve a valuable function by putting focused, specific information at our fingertips.

These messages are typically termed as permission-based, and they allow you to connect with customers and prospects in a direct, intimate fashion unlike many other potential tactics.

Email produces quick results.

Crafting an effective email can take time. But deploying an email and measuring the results can happen rather quickly. Most times, you'll know within about 48 hours if your message hit the mark. This could come in the form of downloads, clicks, purchases, or other metrics that you designate. Whatever you choose to measure, the results will speak for themselves in a relatively short amount of time.

People deal with email.

I think most people prefer not to have a cluttered inbox if they can help it. At some point, your message is likely to be opened, deleted, or filed away.

Granted, you want your email to be highly relevant. You want your audience to open it and take the action you desire. But this doesn't always happen. Even if someone chooses to delete your message before opening it, they will still have to evaluate it in some way. Seeing that a message came from you isn't the worst thing. Over time, if you continue to deliver quality information, you may find that your message hits their inbox at just the right moment when they have a need or interest.

As a last resort, for people that never seem to open your messages, you can lay your cards on the table. Ask them if there is something you could be doing better or if they really want to continue receiving your emails. Worst case, you take someone off your list that doesn't really want to be there.

Email creates a bridge to your content.
One of the most obvious benefits of email is that you can link to just about any online resource you have. If someone gets engaged with your message, they can jump immediately to your content or offer directly from your message.

Email can be segmented.
Even with the simplest email utilities, you can choose to send different messages to different segments of your list. Segmentation can be very simple or highly sophisticated, depending on your needs and nuances of your audience. The power to segment allows you to deliver highly relevant content to subsets of your list that are most likely to respond to each unique message or offer.

You can personalize it.
Beyond simple segmentation, you can also choose to

personalize emails. Personalization tends to drive greater engagement as a general rule. Sure, adding someone's first name to a salutation is a great start. But integrating specific, targeted information that could affect their business can take your campaign to the next level.

Email is relatively inexpensive.

Once you've invested in the up front costs of a marketing automation tool or email service, sending emails is one of the least costly methods for communicating directly with your audience.

How this applied to Readmissions Analytics:

For this campaign, email was the rocket fuel that helped us to drive initial downloads of ebooks, draw in blog readers, and identify initial prospects.

Using Hubspot as our marketing automation tool, we were able to create and deploy many different emails that supported all aspects of the campaign, including:

• Promotion of new ebooks, articles, and other assets.

• Personalized messaging to key prospects.

•Notification of event attendance and speaking engagements.

• Webinar registrations.

The Content Driven Product Launch

It was beneficial that we started out with a robust email list as a foundation for our efforts. However, our legacy house list contained mainly hospital financial contacts. While this was a great starting point, we also needed to reach new personas such as individuals who worked in quality or clinical areas.

Our inbound program helped to supplement the list with permission-based contacts. Through social media, search engine traffic, and conferences, we were able to attract new people to our assets from among these personas. Once they downloaded an ebook or comparable asset, we were able to include them in other outbound email campaigns moving forward.

Earlier, I talked about how we integrated the specific readmissions penalty for different hospitals into personalized emails that went out to targeted contacts. This penalty number represented more than a generalization. It was a specific pain point for their institution that they could not escape and may not have even seen, before we made them aware of it. Not only was this tactic provocative, it set the foundation for establishing the ROI of our product by helping them to reduce this penalty over the long term.

Slideshare

Slideshare

Slideshare.net is a hosting service where you can post presentations, infographics, documents, and videos. According to Slideshare, they receive over 70 million visitors each month and they are one of the top 100 most-visited websites in the world.

Strikingly, *The State of B2B Marketing Report 2015* by Regalix reported that only 17% of marketers utilize Slideshare for product launches. This represents a dramatic opportunity for driving valuable traffic to key content and developing tangible leads.

Why does Slideshare work?

Slideshare presentations drive search results.
Slideshare is a highly trafficked website and enjoys an impressive domain authority. If you've set your presentation up correctly when loading it to Slideshare, paying attention to the relevant keywords, then you should start to see your presentation show up in related search engine results before too long. When I've embedded Slideshare presentations on a blog post, I've seen results for both my blog post and Slideshare presentation appear on the same results screen. There's nothing like getting twice

the bang for your buck.

Slideshare makes repurposing content a snap.

We all have slides hanging around from a customer presentation or webinar. Dust them off, and with a little sprucing up, you can begin sharing that content with a much wider audience. It's a great way to get your content marketing off the ground and prove its value to internal constituents and potential authors.

File formats are suitable for mere mortals.

At a minimum, you can use PowerPoint to create slides that get noticed on Slideshare. Most everyone can put together a slide deck and have it look decent, even if you're not a graphics expert. Slideshare is also great for hosting PDFs, so think white papers, infographics, and other high-value content. The more time you take to thoughtfully prepare your presentation material and make it look good, the better chance it has of standing out on Slideshare. Invest in the look and quality of the material as your resources allow.

Social sharing is easy.

The buzz about social selling is everywhere. Of course, the fastest route to sharing material online is by curating relevant third-party material. But, if you're determined to build trust, and ultimately, relationships with prospects, then it's essential to let your own expertise shine. Once you have great content on Slideshare, it's easy to share it on

Twitter, LinkedIn, or just about anywhere else. In fact, Slideshare presentations can be easily added to LinkedIn profiles and played directly within Twitter.

Slideshare presentations embed easily into websites.

As I mentioned above, embedding Slideshare presentations into your website or other websites is a snap. The advantage to embedding a Slideshare presentation is that the user has more ways to interact with it than if you just linked to a static presentation from your site. For instance, they can scroll the presentation within the page itself, make the presentation full-screen, interact with lead development forms, and more.

Slideshare presentations are valuable to those searching for topical content.

I've personally used information found in Slideshare presentations from other authors to help me think through subjects, persuade others, and source material for stage presentations. I've talked with other B2B marketing professionals who have done the same. The fact that Slideshare presentations show up in search results makes it even more likely that someone researching a topic will stumble across your material and spend time interacting with it.

You can get leads from Slideshare.

Slideshare allows you to setup a simple lead generation

form directly within your presentation. You can choose where in the presentation you would like the form to appear. This service also integrates with Hubspot and Marketo if you wish to bring leads directly into those systems. Keep in mind, this is a paid service that Slideshare offers, but it's not very expensive compared to other channels and has the potential to deliver highly engaged prospects.

You can link to anything.

You can embed links to other websites, forms, and other assets directly within the content of your Slideshare presentation. You can also include links using services like Click To Tweet which allows users to post information from your presentation directly to Twitter, for instance. You can link to just about anything after the third slide in your presentation.

How this applied to Readmissions Analytics:

Slideshare became an important component of the Readmissions Analytics campaign. Oddly enough, we didn't host presentations there for this particular campaign. However, it did become a repository for several documents, a video, and an infographic.

The first resource we loaded there was an infographic that broke down several key statistics related to the readmissions program from Medicare. The infographic was entitled, *Why you should care about the Medicare Hospital Readmissions Reduction Program.* We produced the infographic at the early stages of the campaign to bring attention to the problem since it was so new for our hospital customers.

Posting the infographic to Slideshare was a no-brainer. First, the keywords associated with it helped to drive organic traffic on Slideshare directly. It also gave us a convenient way to share the infographic on Twitter, LinkedIn, and through embedded material on our website and those of our partners.

Next, once our explainer video was produced, we posted that to Slideshare as well. At the initial phase of the launch, I customized our page on Slideshare so that the explainer video was the featured asset at the top of the page.

The True Financial Impact of Hospital Readmissions article was an important asset for us. Making this in-depth piece available on Slideshare helped us to drive organic traffic to it, and we were able to embed it on our website and share on social media very easily. The main author also added the article to his LinkedIn profile as another way to promote it to his network.

Other articles were published periodically in local chapter newsletters of related professional organizations, and we posted those to Slideshare as well.

Our first ebook was posted to Slideshare. I allowed public access to it, but never promoted it since it was typically only available by filling out a form on our website. This was more of an experiment than anything else, just to see how it would perform without any attention. Overall, it garnered over 400 views. For such a niche topic, this wasn't too bad.

The most successful asset we loaded to Slideshare was probably the least impressive piece we produced. As I detailed in the section on "blogs", the one-page worksheet for how to calculate the LACE Risk Score has generated over 22,000 views. In this case, most of that traffic came from our website via it being embedded on the related blog post. But almost half came from organic traffic to Slideshare directly.

Bear in mind, a short worksheet is not the typical in-depth content that usually works well on Slideshare. But in this instance, it was very useful to the audience who craved that material.

Social Media

Social Media

It's hard to escape social media as a marketing tactic in this day and age. However, social media may represent the largest opportunity for marketing misalignment today.

The proliferation of channels and the speed at which they change is somewhat overwhelming. Unlike more mature marketing tactics that are well understood, social media presents a range of new challenges for marketers and business owners to manage.

When selecting social media channels to participate in, you should:

1. Ensure that your audience actually uses a given platform.

2. Consider if the platform is a good fit for your brand.

3. Set realistic expectations for your level of participation on a platform and specific goals for what you want to achieve there.

If you look around on social media sites, you'll see a graveyard of open accounts that lie dormant, contain outdated posts, or have no business being there in the first place. It usually takes only minutes (or seconds) to open a social media account. It's much harder to sustain a presence, let alone produce a tangible impact.

Each social media platform has its own unique user base,

focus, and methods for members to communicate with one another. Sure, individuals and businesses use multiple social media sites, but what they accomplish on each differs depending on the platform.

From a strategic point of view, my first recommendation is to identify which platforms your current or potential customers are utilizing. That sounds basic, but it's easy to start out by thinking that you need to participate on many social media sites to be successful, and that's not true. In fact, the smaller your organization, the more focused your efforts should be on fewer sites where you engage more actively. Spreading yourself too thin will guarantee that you won't get results anywhere.

Research the social media platforms you are interested in and see if those types of people are active there and interacting on topics that are relevant to your business. I say this specifically, because context is very important to your initiatives. For instance, you may find that several individuals from your target customer base are active on Facebook. However, if they mainly interact with their personal networks, they might not be interested in your business message there. However, they may have a completely different reaction if you were to reach out on LinkedIn. Again, this may or may not be true depending on the circumstances.

After you've established the proper user context, you have to ask yourself if the platform is a fit for your brand. Establishing a user base is one element in determining this. But you have to decide if the platform is aligned with the tone of your brand, your mission, and so on. Some criteria you can use to help evaluate a fit are:

Types of content you plan to share

If video is not in your plan, then video-sharing platforms are probably out. Do you produce a lot of still images you can share? Then image-sharing platforms might be in. Having a content strategy that aligns with each platform's content focus will ensure that you can maintain a robust presence there and grow your following.

Frequency of communication

Honestly, for social media to work, you have to communicate pretty frequently no matter which platform you are on. However, platforms like Twitter demand that you interact more frequently and connect in conversations more personally to be successful.

Platform focus – business, personal, or both

Some platforms, like LinkedIn, are almost exclusively professionally oriented. Others, like Facebook, are used more by individuals to keep in touch with their personal networks or enhance their personal knowledge. Then you have platforms like Twitter that cross into both the personal and professional. Alignment is the key here as well. If it feels inappropriate to interact with your target customers about a topic on a particular network, then it's probably best not to do so.

Why does social media work?

Social media ROI can be notoriously difficult to quantify. Just because someone "likes" your post, doesn't necessarily mean that will translate into business. A lot of small businesses get involved in social media and then give up because they can't justify the investment to themselves.

Often, this stems from a lack of setting conversion goals to understand if their investment is leading to the actions that they desire. Like any other tactic, social media requires a strategy and a commitment to execution and measurement for it to be truly successful.

I've worked in complex B2B niches for most of my career. In many cases, the customers I've served didn't use social media too often for professional purposes. It's not good enough for someone to have a profile on a platform; they actually need to visit it with some frequency to see your message.

Regardless, there are a few good reasons why maintaining a presence on social media is still beneficial, even in markets where people don't interact widely on it.

People notice.
Any professional who works in social media is striving to create engagement. You want your target audience to click through to your content, like, follow, retweet, and so on. These are often the basic units of measurement to decide if

a campaign or a particular post was successful.

However, many users are casual observers. They may visit social media sites, but they are only inclined to view posts and not necessarily take action.

But here's the thing - they may not like or follow you, but those that visit relevant social media sites will notice your presence there. This sounds like a weak argument for old-fashioned branding, but it's true nonetheless. If you're not active, you won't get seen. If you are there, you'll look sharp and on the ball.

Over time, your audience will come to appreciate the value you bring if you are delivering great content and they will more than likely start interacting with it in some way. The key is that you have to manage the time you put into curating posts so that you can maximize your exposure without draining your resources.

Visibility is not a substitute for engagement, but being regularly active on social media can produce intangible benefits that you'll realize over the long term.

You can link to your content.

Social media allows you to link directly to your content through posts. This can be an important way to draw people into your fold, even if the click-through rate on any given post is low. You can create several different posts leading to the same piece of content and strategically repeat them in your schedule so that you consistently promote key content.

Many social media platforms including LinkedIn, Facebook, and Twitter offer opportunities to promote your posts through paid options. This can help you broaden the reach of your posts beyond your current roster of followers and specifically target the kinds of people you want to reach.

By introducing these new audiences to your valuable content, you have the potential to start long-term relationships with them that could eventually lead to them becoming paid customers.

You can support sales activities.

Successful salespeople are always striving to deliver value to their customers and prospects. In today's world, one of the ways they can demonstrate their knowledge and give their audience valuable information in advance of asking for a sale is for them to engage on social media.

Salespeople who have taken the time to build connections with important influencers and decision-makers on social media are literally sitting on a goldmine. I've found that in some cases, while these same key individuals are reticent to engage with corporate social media accounts, they will connect with a salesperson they've come to like and trust. This means that as a marketer, you can reach a whole new group of highly targeted, extremely valuable contacts by motivating your sales team to share your content with their networks.

There are different ways you can go about operationalizing how salespeople share content. These range from asking them to share directly from corporate accounts to staging your posts in an employee advocacy platform like Gaggle AMP that makes it simple for them to share content across networks.

The benefits of creating a synergy with your sales team around social media are enormous. Their social networks give you a new conduit for distributing your content. Sales teams benefit by building authority and deepening relationships with their most important customers and prospects. In other words, the sometimes elusive goal of aligning sales and marketing activities becomes more achievable.

How this applied to Readmissions Analytics

You may have guessed by now that our target audience of hospital finance and clinical professionals was not wildly active on social media. Nonetheless, we decided to amp up our presence on LinkedIn and Twitter to support the product launch for some very specific reasons.

When it came to LinkedIn, we could tell pretty quickly that a good census of our target audience was present on the platform. This didn't necessarily translate to them being actively engaged, but they at least had profiles there and that was a good start.

Twitter was not as promising. There appeared to be very little activity from our audience on that platform. However, our Twitter strategy had a little less to do with what happened on the platform than it did with how we decided to leverage the feed.

The effort was fueled by our own content mingled with curated third-party material. This gave us the ability to promote our proprietary expertise while demonstrating broader thought leadership by sharing key articles and other content of use to our audience.

Beyond our corporate Twitter feed and LinkedIn company page, we elicited the help of our sales team to spread the message via their own social networks. To do this, we selected the Gaggle AMP platform. This tool aggregated content from our corporate social media accounts and blog so that our sales team always had on-message content at their fingertips to share. Each time a new post appeared, each sales representative received an email, allowing them to share the post with just one click.

This approach had several benefits. For one, it positioned our sales representatives as thought leaders in front of their own networks around the readmissions issue and kept them top of mind, as they all posted regularly. Second, it helped us to reach people over social media who may not have been visiting our corporate properties. And finally, we were able to measure the impact that our sales representatives had on engagement with our assets.

We chose to sponsor posts on LinkedIn that promoted core content assets. This delivered thousands of impressions and many downloads from target personas relevant to the readmissions offering.

While we maintained an active Twitter presence, engagement never really took off there. However, we did embed several posts into a weekly news round-up on our blog. This gave us additional content to share each week and it took about ten minutes to create and publish each post.

Our website also had a widget for our Twitter feed. This brought fresh content onto the site throughout the day and at the very minimum, made us look like we were on top of things. While not an optimal way to measure social media, I can tell you that over time, people did notice what we were doing across platforms. During sales calls and other face-to-face encounters, customers and prospects began to mention how robust our presence was and how much they appreciated it. The customers we served looked on us more favorably and our internal stakeholders felt positive about what we were doing.

They key to our whole social media program during this period was that most of it was managed in about one hour per week. We had our hands full creating content and managing other aspects of the campaign. Social media just couldn't take up the majority of our time, particularly since its utility and ROI was as yet unproven.

In the next section, I'll talk about some of my personal curation strategies so you can see for yourself that maintaining a social media presence doesn't necessarily have to be a daunting task.

Techniques for curating third party content

Sharing content from multiple third-party sources is a great way to get going on social media quickly. But visiting each source site every time you want to prepare social media posts will cost you a lot of time.

Enter RSS feeds.

RSS (Really Simple Syndication) allows you to aggregate and organize content from multiple online sources into a single channel. Essentially, you will be feeding content directly into one interface, allowing you to quickly review articles of interest and select the ones you want to post.

At the office, I work on a desktop. Microsoft Outlook is my constant companion and it is able to accept RSS feeds directly. So for aggregating content that I post professionally, I use Outlook.

I have a separate Outlook folder setup for the feeds I monitor, and as new posts publish from those sources, the folder fills up. On Fridays, when I'm ready to stage my social media posts for the coming week, I expand the folder containing the RSS feeds and literally dozens of articles are available for me to choose from. They look just like email previews, so I can quickly scan headlines to select the articles that might be worth sharing and delete the ones that are not the right fit.

Adding a new RSS feed to Outlook is as simple as right clicking on the RSS folder and entering the URL of the feed which will usually look something like this: www.launchcatalyst.net/feed

To aggregate content that I post to my personal social media accounts, I use Feedly. Feedly is a great tool for organizing and discovering new content. I like Feedly because it has a very user-friendly iPad app, so I can browse and stage content whether I'm sitting on the couch or on the go. Feedly connects directly with social media platforms like Facebook and Twitter so you can post directly to them or you can stage posts through apps like Buffer or utilize other iOS sharing options.

RSS feeds supply me with plenty of articles to choose from. However, I also like to look for content in sources that I may not capture regularly. Twitter is great for this purpose.

There are different strategies for discovering content on Twitter. Searching for a topic using a hashtag is an easy way to start. Hashtags in Twitter simply help to organize tweets relevant to a particular topic or conversation.

To track tweets from a particular set of sources, you'll want to create a Twitter list. A list will let you look at tweets only from sources relevant to the list you created. For instance, I could create a list called "B2B Marketing" and select to include specific accounts that tweet about that topic. When I view the list, I'll just see the latest tweets from resources I trust for B2B Marketing.

If I'm just generally curious about top sources around a given topic, I'll search Google. This is not the best way to aggregate content regularly, but it can help you uncover deep, authoritative content and locate new sources that you could potentially track through feeds or on Twitter. You could also set up Google alerts to get notified when something happens related to a keyword or phrase that's important to you.

Scheduling content for social media

As I identify content that I want to share on social media, I immediately schedule it. At work, I use Hubspot for marketing automation. I have their Chrome extension installed so I can simply press a button in my browser and schedule a post on the fly.

To save time, I will usually stage the same tweet for release 2-3 times over the course of a week. It's common knowledge that tweets don't last a particularly long time, so tweeting the same content a few different times is not a problem as you won't reach most of your audience at any given moment. I do make a concerted effort to change the wording in the tweets and experiment with new hashtags to make each tweet stand out.

LinkedIn is the other major platform we use at my organization, so while I'm creating the tweet, I'll use the same Hubspot interface to create a LinkedIn post. Since we update our LinkedIn company page a little less frequently than Twitter, I try to be more selective about the articles I share there.

Remember, in addition to scheduling posts using third-party

content, you should share your own content as well. At work when I'm using Hubspot, I can quickly review prior posts that had good engagement and select to repost them. I use this to help me recirculate my core content regularly.

With this process, I can easily schedule enough content to fill our social media accounts for a week.

For my personal social media presence, I use Buffer. I generally discover content on Feedly and Twitter, then I use the Buffer app on my iPad to stage posts day-to-day directly from those applications.

Like Hubspot and most other social media scheduling programs, Buffer will allow you to post to multiple social media accounts. To make things easy, I schedule posts for Twitter, Facebook and LinkedIn through Buffer.

That's it. It takes about an hour each week to prepare social media posts for BESLER's corporate account and 15-20 minutes each night staging content for my personal accounts.

Beyond posting, social media works best when you're, well, social. This means you'll also want to devote time to commenting on posts, liking content, and exchanging messages when appropriate. If you carve out a few minutes a day for that activity, social media can enhance your business without putting a drain on your most precious resource, time.

Exhibits & Conferences

Exhibits & Conferences

Industry exhibits are a mainstay in B2B marketing. They act as a sort of "speed dating" situation where you can physically meet and talk to many potential and current customers in a day or two.

Exhibits are also a good forum to reinforce your brand message, introduce new products quickly to a large group, and test concepts ranging from potential new products to marketing messages.

In this section, we'll examine why exhibits are a good outlet for leveraging your core content and how you can do that.

Why do exhibits and conferences work?

They allow targeted distribution of content.

Often, content is dispersed when someone responds to an inbound or outbound marketing initiative. Personally, one of the most frustrating things I find about inbound marketing is that people who are not prime targets can download assets and enter your funnel only to get screened out later on. This could be because they are not decision-makers, they are from competitive firms, they are students and so on.

At an exhibition, the tables are turned a bit. Since most conferences attract certain types of personas, you know that you are bound to encounter a fair share of high-quality prospects, provided the conference aligns well with your target audience. Of course, not all conferences attract decision-makers. However, you may network with individuals who could influence a purchasing decision or bring back information to those who can make a decision.

There are several distribution options, but don't forget about print!

These days, much of the content we create is delivered digitally. And you can still deliver your content digitally at an exhibition through mobile applications and the like.

There is also an opportunity at conferences to turn your digital assets into print matter that can be available at your booth, distributed in bag drops, and given out strategically by sales people.

Conference organizers usually offer many paid distribution options for circulating your content among attendees. Look them over ahead of time. You might find one that's right for you.

Brand reinforcement.

If you already have an active content marketing program, then offering your content at an exhibition is a natural extension of how you already provide value to your audience. If your audience is used to reading your blog posts and downloading your papers, then giving them something new at a conference to help educate them will only serve to reinforce the image you've worked hard to cultivate.

If you give your visitors a high value asset, either digitally or in print, you'll leave them with a positive impression and something that they can interact with long after the conference is over.

If you're new to the content marketing landscape, what better way to introduce people to your brand than to give them something important they can take with them.

There is a natural bridge from content to post-show follow-up.

Making the follow-up call after a conference can be challenging. You know going in that attendees will be swamped with post-show offers, emails, phone calls, and direct mail.

While everyone wants to close business as a result of hot leads they developed at an exhibition, following up to see if someone liked the content you gave them could be a less threatening approach to start out with. If your goal is to form the basis for a relationship, then this may be the most practical way to go.

If your prospect forgot about the content you gave them (and let's face it, many people probably will after the tornado of conference activities and travel), you can offer to resend it and jumpstart the conversation without asking for a sale right then and there.

<u>Try out your content live and derive new content.</u>
If you are fortunate enough to secure a speaking engagement at a conference, then you have the perfect platform for conveying your core content ideas to a dedicated audience.

You could easily extract key points from a white paper, for instance, to use in your presentation and then point attendees to your booth or website to get the full report.

In the section of this book that discussed speaking engagements, I noted that you can also take advantage of new speaker slides or notes as a basis for creating new content deliverables. That is low-hanging fruit you definitely don't want to pass up.

How this applied to Readmissions Analytics

The simplest thing that we did to support our readmissions offering at exhibitions was to print the two ebooks we created. The printed versions made for impressive, attractive deliverables that we distributed at our booths and carried along to conferences that our representatives attended, but where they did not exhibit.

As I mentioned earlier in this book, we blew up an infographic we created into a large standing display that we placed on the outside corner of our booth property. This display naturally attracted attention as people stopped to read the variety of information on it.

We did not set out to use the infographic at our booths when we made the infographic originally, but the idea bubbled up during a planning meeting, and it made perfect sense. Look for ways to extract facts, bullets, and other information from your content to create similar displays and you'll not only reinforce your brand, you'll get more mileage from deliverables and provide valuable information to your audience in a different context.

In situations where we had speaking engagements happening during an exhibition, we were sure to mention that attendees could visit our booth for more information. After an hour-long session that educated them on all of the facets of the readmissions issue, there was a built-in conduit for driving traffic to our booth so attendees could pick up copies of our ebooks.

Partnerships and Sponsorships

Partnerships and Sponsorships

When deploying a content marketing program, it helps to leverage every potential distribution point that you can.

One way to increase the volume of your distribution is to work with partners who cater to the same or similar audiences that you wish to attract. Depending on the nature of your relationship, this could be through some type of mutually beneficial exchange ("I'll promote your content to my audience if you promote my content to yours") or it could be through a paid sponsorship of some kind.

Perhaps the first thing to remember about partnerships is that most people won't promote your content out of the goodness of their heart. You'll either have to offer something valuable in exchange, or you'll have to pay to reach their audience (what I would call a sponsorship). If you consider this when going in, you'll avoid disappointment when the other party asks for something in return.

This may sound pretty basic, but I've seen senior level people become confused and almost crushed, when asked to open up their wallet to reach the audience of a potential partner. In those cases, I think they believed that their content or product offering had something beneficial for the partner's audience and that the partner would be doing their audience a service by telling them about it.

The reality is that organizations that have taken the time and energy to build and cultivate a loyal audience have done so to create a foundation for their business. They will seek ways to monetize that relationship over time and are not usually inclined to provide access to that audience for free to another party. They will look for some type of mutually beneficial exchange or financial remuneration. However, there are a few exceptions, as you'll see.

Why do partnerships and sponsorships work?

They reach new targeted prospects.
Simply put, working with partners can help you reach new potential prospects faster than you might be able to reach them through your own marketing efforts. Since your partners already have a built-in audience, they can use their own promotional vehicles to promote your content to them directly.

Even if you are a well known entity in a market segment and have a solid working prospect database, it's likely that you won't have a 100% overlap with the audience of a sponsor organization. You're bound to uncover new prospects and, as an added benefit, you can reinforce your message with people in your current audience.

You can enter new market segments.

Partners can accelerate your entrance into new market segments. If the product or service you are launching appeals to a customer base with which you do not have previous experience, then working with a partner who knows the space can help you make inroads quicker.

Beyond the immediate benefit of leveraging their dedicated audience and communication conduits, partners can help you learn about marketplace concerns and trends, and help you shape market messages, product features, and points of differentiation. Partners may have deep relationships with key influencers who can provide consultation and facilitate networking with other important market players.

Partners may lend credibility to your content.

If you are working with a well-respected partner organization, the fact that they are promoting your content can confer a degree of credibility that might otherwise take you time to build up on your own with a new audience.

Assuming that your partner organization respects their audience and delivers consistent value to them, then their audience would have every reason to believe that they would only receive quality information from them. In an environment with no lack of available content for prospects to choose from, this tactic can help you break through the noise.

How this applied to Readmissions Analytics

At BESLER, there were existing partnerships that could be exploited and new ones were formed to promote Readmissions Analytics.

One long-standing relationship involved the sponsorship/partnership of a popular blog that reached a portion of our target audience. As part of the relationship, our partner promoted our content assets to their audience on their blog resources section, highlighted key deliverables on their home page, and promoted our social media posts on their channels.

Other existing relationships included several hospital associations throughout the country. These organizations promoted our content through their websites, e-newsletters, and social media. They also worked with us to deliver content directly to their members in the form of webinars and group meetings.

A new relationship we formed was with a hyper-targeted, niche publication that dealt only with the readmissions topic. Their audience was small, but extremely focused. We started out by contracting with them to send an email to their audience list on our behalf promoting one of our ebooks.

As they became familiar with our content, they realized how much it dovetailed with the content they delivered to their audience. This particular publication relied on third-party contributions heavily and they began to integrate some of our content on their website and e-newsletter. For instance, they embedded one of our YouTube videos on their website and promoted that through social media and across their other channels.

As time went on, they also published articles we contributed and asked us to keep them coming.

This example represents a situation where a mutually beneficial exchange occurred that did not always involve the exchange of money. In this case, the publisher did not ask for compensation to distribute our content after our initial email blast. They were happy to use it strategically as part of their program because it fit with their mission as a publisher and benefitted their paid subscription audience. Of course, they still looked for ways to help us boost some our content through advertising, but they found enough value in our content arsenal that we both benefited from their distribution of it.

Another approach that we took to help amplify our distribution may look a bit more like advertising since it was a paid placement. But it was much more dynamic. In this instance, we worked with a major publisher in our space to syndicate one of our ebooks. This package included hosting the ebook on their website for several months, promoting it heavily to their large list through direct email blasts and banners in their daily e-newsletter, and frequent social media posts.

This approach opened up our content to a much wider audience than we could reach on our own. It also delivered a sustained presence of a key piece of our content in front of a highly targeted audience. This effort yielded several hundred downloads of the ebook. While it was the most expensive placement we conducted in the entire campaign, it yielded tangible results.

Conclusion and Results

There is no doubt that executing an effective and sustainable content marketing campaign requires many moving pieces to come together harmoniously. I hope that through the course of this book, I've demonstrated that if you begin with a clear vision, leverage the expertise you have, and build a core set of content assets to support your initiative, it doesn't take a huge team or a massive budget to execute a good campaign.

There are a few things that I think made the campaign successful beyond quantitative results alone:

Strategy came before tactics.
From the beginning, the campaign was designed to circle around a core set of focused content objectives. The tactics were subservient to the content message, which focused on overcoming specific market obstacles and developing a logical segue to our solution. Only after our objectives were set and our messaging was clear did we set about articulating our message across a wide variety of media.

We engaged our target audience in novel ways.
Our target market was simply not used to being educated and engaged by a vendor in the manner in which we approached them. From video to Slideshare and speaking engagements to ebooks, our message was available,

consistent, and visible to our prospects in a variety of formats. We noticed a distinct difference in the tone of our exhibits, for instance, when we had to drive back to headquarters to get more printouts of our ebook because we blew through our inventory in the first hour of a major show.

Salespeople reported that customers they talked to mentioned how well-regarded and helpful our educational material was and how that really elevated the perception of our firm in their eyes.

Our internal experts evolved into amazing content creators.

We had absolutely zero content on readmissions when we started. Moreover, our internal experts had never been called on to write ebooks, go on speaking tours or anything like that. Yet in just a few short months we turned out numerous assets that generated thousands of downloads and web visits contributing to a robust pipeline.

Results quickly displaced any lingering skepticism about the value of content marketing for launching a new product.

Repurposing content was a force multiplier.

There is no way we could have deployed a content marketing program with this many components by reinventing new content for every single deliverable we needed.

We videotaped speaking engagements which we then used to create a series of YouTube videos, blog articles, and social media posts. We wrote ebooks and then broke them up into blog articles and interview guides for podcasts. We put our articles, worksheets, and infographics on Slideshare.

The point is that we centered our content around a set of specific messages, and then built core assets to convey that message. Each core asset could then be leveraged in multiple formats to get our message out.

There were several quantitative measures that also demonstrated the value of the sales and marketing effort. Around the time this campaign won the 2015 B2B Bright Bulb Award, the stats were:

• Over a quarter million dollars in the pipeline (product price approximately $25k-$45k)

• 40 face-to-face product demos held or booked

• 1,000 e-book downloads

• 16,500 page views of blog articles

• 17,700 views of assets on Slideshare

• 820 views of YouTube videos

• 114 new contacts generated representing key personas we had not targeted previously

• 119 new double opt-in subscribers to our blog

• Published articles reaching thousands of targeted readers

The Content Driven Product Launch

•Multiple speaking engagements building thought leadership across our market

While content marketing can work for every size business, it was my goal to demonstrate how small to mid-size B2B businesses can go about developing and deploying content campaigns to get results. It takes vision along with a committed effort, but the results you can achieve are truly amazing.

If you'd like to see some of the campaign elements for yourself, visit

launchcatalyst.net/contentdrivenproductlaunch

Good luck!

Michael Passanante

About the Author

Michael Passanante has two decades of experience launching products and services into B2B markets. He has held a variety of positions in marketing, product management, and sales in multibillion-dollar global organizations and smaller privately owned companies. He holds an MBA in Management and a BS in Marketing from Rutgers University. Michael resides with his family in southern New Jersey.

Visit **launchcatalyst.net** for additional resources and insights to make your product launches explosive!

LinkedIn: linkedin.com/in/michaelpassanante

Twitter: @launch_catalyst

If you liked this book, please visit Amazon.com to leave a positive review. Thank you!

The Content Driven Product Launch

www.ingramcontent.com/pod-product-compliance
Lightning Source LLC
Chambersburg PA
CBHW070322190526
45169CB00005B/1709